Wellington Clayton Wendell, Ida A. Wendell

Miscellaneous Poems

Wellington Clayton Wendell, Ida A. Wendell
Miscellaneous Poems
ISBN/EAN: 9783744713856
Printed in Europe, USA, Canada, Australia, Japan
Cover: Foto ©Thomas Meinert / pixelio.de

More available books at **www.hansebooks.com**

Miscellaneous Poems:

OR,

LEISURE HOURS.

BY

WELLINGTON C. WENDELL.

EDITED BY HIS DAUGHTER.

ALBANY N. Y.:
JOEL MUNSELL.
1875.

TO

MY DEAR MOTHER,

MRS. ADDIE S. WENDELL,

AS A TOKEN OF LOVE,

THIS

VOLUME IS AFFECTIONATELY

Dedicated.

Preface.

Though literature was not, with my beloved father, a profession, the ensuing pages will bear testimony that his brain was not an idle one. Modest as was his own estimate of his abilities, he more than once expressed a purpose, whenever the convenient time should come, to gather his published and other written productions into a small printed volume. Had he lived to execute this design, it is not unlikely that, in the work of selecting, he would have cast aside some effusions to which the partial love and less severe taste of survivors willingly accord a permanent place, side by side with the worthiest things that he ever wrote.

A considerable number of the pieces which are here brought together have appeared in print as newspaper contributions. Some of them, as occasion demanded, were published in other forms. Others still were dashed off to beguile a "leisure hour," or entertain a friend.

The fact of the appearance of this unpretentious volume is not solely due to the remembered purpose noted above, nor yet to the partial love of an only child. An instinctive prompting would of course incite her to the duty of gathering together and arranging, for convenience of reference and permanent preservation, the written productions of the dear departed one. But their present embodiment in book form is in great measure the result of the known wishes of many relatives and friends.

Nothing need be claimed for the contents of this little volume on the score of poetic merit. Few if any of those who see it will be in the least disposed to criticise. It will for the most part be perused by loving friends. If merit there be, these will find it; if faults, they will easily pardon and forget them.

In the work of selection and arrangement, I have received valuable assistance and counsel from my honored grandfather, Jacob Wendell, Esq.

Rev. Rufus Wendell has kindly supervised the proof reading, as the sheets were passing through the press, and has also prepared the " In Memoriam" sketches contained in the volume.

For all assistance received in this labor of love, I wish to express my sincere thanks.

IDA A. WENDELL.

ALBANY, May 1, 1875.

In Memoriam.

WELLINGTON CLAYTON WENDELL, eldest son of Jacob and Margaret F. Wendell, was born in Fort Plain, N. Y., on the 30th day of January, 1832.

When about seventeen years of age he entered the office of the village paper, the *Montgomery Phœnix*, as an apprentice to the printing business. He completed his apprenticeship in due course, and became an excellent practical printer.

He was married February 16, 1852, to Miss ADELINE S. CLOVER, of Springfield, N. Y., an estimable lady of English parentage. IDA A., their only child, was born July 14, 1856.

Early in 1854, the subject of this sketch associated with himself as partner a former fellow-apprentice, Mr. Harrison Stansel, and purchased the *Phœnix* establishment. The firm at once changed the name of the paper, and on March 9, 1854, issued the first number of the *Mohawk Valley Register*. Mr. Wendell's proprietary connection with the paper (with two successive changes in the style of the firm) continued until May, 1859, when he sold his interest and removed to Albany. His withdrawal from the *Register* was chronicled by his partner, C. W. Webster, Esq., in the following editorial " Personal " : —

"As will be noticed by the perusal of the following card, Mr. Wendell, our late partner, has disposed of his property in the office of the *Register* to Mr. Crounse, and severs his pecuniary interest in the establishment, with the present issue. Mr. Wendell's connection with the paper dates from the very first number, and ours from an early period in the third volume. During our partnership, we have at all times found him an efficient coadjutor in the department over which he had supervision, and feel that our readers and patrons are in no small degree indebted to him, not only for the mechanical skill which has at all times been apparent in his work, but also for the faculty, often exercised, of selecting from the mass of reading, for the edification and entertainment of our subscribers. An intimacy of three years, in close business relations, has engendered feelings which make it a source of deep regret to have severed — and in his new 'voyage,' we bespeak for him kindly winds, a clear sky, and every anticipation of a buoyant hope."

The "Card" of Mr. Wendell, alluded to in the foregoing kindly paragraph, was as follows : —

"With the present number the connection of the undersigned with the *Register* ceases; and in parting company with the noble vessel that has borne us for the past five years, it befits us to render it due meed of praise for the gallant manner in which it has out-ridden many a storm, withstood the buffetings of ill-winds and high seas, and moored us in safe anchorage at the end of the cruise. With right for our compass, a desire to please for our chart, and a good subscription list for ballast, the angry sea was despoiled of its power, and the voyage rendered pleasant. As a general thing, we have found the winter of doubt and anxious expectancy, succeeded by the spring-time of pleasant realization; and although, at times, despondent clouds would dart athwart our path, yet the "silver lining" would buoy us up and bid us be of good cheer.

It is the province of friends and patrons to render judgment, in our case, as to duty done; but few can chide us with not essaying to the extent of our feeble power, to fulfil the obligations which our position imposed upon us. In our patrons we have found many friends for whom it proved a pleasure to cater, and whose magnanimity, beneficence and kindly words have often led us to bright oases in the desert of life.

While it is painful to part with such friends, it is gratifying to know that we leave the *Register* in able hands, who will not fail to make it still more worthy of popular favor and support. The fine taste and sound judgment of our partner will still continue to be weekly reflected in its columns; and he will spare no pains or labor to maintain the high character of the paper.

In our successor, Mr. Crounse,[1] the friends of the *Register* will find a gentleman every way worthy of their confidence and patronage; and we trust that in each of them he may find an open heart, ready to give him a cordial and profitable greeting.

May the *Register*, under its new *regime*, become an oak in the forest of papers, and receive sufficient of the " root —— " to render it firm in integrity, unswayed by

---

[1] Hon. Lorenzo Crounse, who is now (1875) serving a second term as member of Congress from Nebraska.

partisan or sectarian factions and creeds, and unawed by the blustering of "little giants;" but may it be resolute in promulgating *right* and *truth*, speedy in uprooting error, and zealous in maintaining an unblemished reputation.

With these few remarks, we bid adieu to our friends, hoping, however, that in dissevering our hand from the press, our friendship shall remain unbroken for the residue of our lives. W. C. WENDELL."

With the exception of two years spent in Philadelphia, Mr. Wendell, after his removal from Fort Plain, resided in Albany to the close of his life.

The first four years were devoted to his trade in the offices of Joel Munsell, Esq., and the *Albany Evening Journal*.

In 1863, he obtained a position in the office of the Provost Marshal General of the State of New York, where he was employed about two years. Once, during the time, he was sent to Washington to adjust the accounts between the Albany office and the general government—a difficult service for the satisfactory performance of which he was handsomely rewarded. On retiring from the office, his chief, Gen. Frederick Townsend, in a written paper voluntarily given, testified in most flattering terms to the ability and fidelity with which he had discharged the duties of his place.

It may, in this connection, be mentioned as unquestionable, that the piece entitled "*The Soldier's*

Good Bye," printed in this volume (pp. 104–106), had its inspiration in the strong impulse to volunteer which was felt by the author during the early part of the war of the rebellion. His warmest sympathies were enlisted in behalf of his beloved country, and it is probable that but for the counsel of friends he would have entered the army.

After leaving the Provost Marshal's office, Mr. Wendell held positions, successively, with the Merchants Union Express Company, J. W. Osborn & Co., the Singer Sewing Machine Company, and Weed, Parsons & Co. In 1870, he removed to Philadelphia, where he was for two years associated with Mr. Frank Hine in the Sewing Machine business. In the spring of 1872, he returned to Albany to accept the position of bookkeeper for Marshall & Wendell, Pianoforte manufacturers, in whose employ he continued to the time of his death.

Mr. Wendell's leisure hours were more or less occupied with the study of inventions, and during his lifetime he obtained letters patent on four inventions of his own — a rubber cushion slate frame, a book cover, a door catch and buffer, and a sewing machine box cover.

On Saturday evening, November 16, 1872, Mr. Wendell was attacked with the illness which resulted in his death. At the close of the day's business — just after he had, with voice and instrument, and with much animation, been executing several popular airs for the entertainment of cousins who had called on him — he repaired to the barber-shop of the City Hotel to be shaved and take a bath. While in the bathing-room he had a sudden and violent attack of spinal meningitis. He was promptly removed in a carriage to his home, and medical aid was at once summoned. After being severely ill for four or five days he began to improve, and on the 27th day of the month he had his physician's permission to undertake a trip to Fort Plain, in order to be present at a Thanksgiving family-gathering on the following day. He stood the journey well, and on the 28th participated with great enjoyment in the festivities of Thanksgiving Day. On the following Monday (Dec. 2) he and his daughter returned to Albany. He had so far recovered that he expected to be able to resume his duties in the counting-room the next morning, and so stated to one of his employers on his way home from the depot. That evening, however, he experienced a violent recurrence of the attack by which he had been prostrated sixteen days previously. His wife returned home the following day. His illness was very severe; he continued to grow worse; and near the hour of midnight on Friday, December 6, 1872, death put an end to the scene.

A loving husband, a tender father, a dutiful son, a warm-hearted and faithful friend, had passed from mortal sight.

During the early part of his illness Mr. Wendell assured his pastor, Rev. Mr. Hulburd, that it had long been his habit to seek the Divine blessing in prayer; referred with great frankness to causes which had kept him back from such an open religious profession as he was convinced duty demanded at his hands; and expressed his firm purpose to assume his proper relation to the church if his life was spared.

Already years have elapsed since the hour of sorrowful separation chronicled in these paragraphs, but many hearts to-day beat quicker at the mention of the name of dear "Welly." He attached himself to his friends with "hooks of steel," and his memory will ever be most affectionately cherished by them all.

The subjoined newspaper articles are given as a fitting close to our brief "In Memoriam." The "Family Gathering," described by Mr. Simms, is the same that is referred to in the above sketch.

From the Canajoharie Radii,

A FAMILY GATHERING.

BY J. R. SIMMS, ESQ., OF FORT PLAIN, N. Y.

A time-honored custom of New England has for a century gathered families together to partake of a Thanksgiving dinner, there being assembled around the same table (groaning under the weight of everything an epicure could desire), not unfrequently, the representatives of three, and sometimes four generations in lineal descent.

This custom does not prevail to any very great extent in Dutch families; but that of Jacob Wendell, Esq., in our village, is an exception to the rule, and whosoever looked into his well-ordered dwelling, on Thursday last, must have imagined himself "where the woodbine twineth," in some cozy house in Yankeedom. There was a family gathering of parents, children and grand-children, numbering all together some fifteen or twenty happy souls.— Besides the heads of the family, or "Old Folks at Home," the company embraced three married sons and their families, one unmarried son, and a son-in-law and family. H. L. Harter, Esq., who married the youngest daughter, is a Professor in the State Normal School at Potsdam, and his duties prevented that couple from meeting at the festive board. All the members of the family present, each writing a sentiment, sent on one sheet a letter of regrets to Prof. Harter and wife for their absence from the circle.

This family has for years observed this New England custom of getting as many of its members as possible at the Thanksgiving dinner table; but it is very probable this may prove the last one they will enjoy in this place One of the sons, Nathan D. Wendell, Esq., Cashier of the Merchants National Bank of Albany, has just been elected Treasurer of Albany County, and it seems not unlikely that he may require his father's services in the discharge of his new duties. Nearly all the family are singers, and when they get together the welkin rings with their happy voices. We enjoyed the pleasure on Thanksgiving Day, of listening to one of those impromptu concerts. The first piece they sang was an Ode written for a similar occasion, and first sung December 7, 1865. It consists of five stanzas, with a chorus, and was written by one of the sons,

W. Clayton Wendell, Esq., who gave it the appropriate title of "*Home, Home Again. Thanksgiving Day*" — set to the air " Ring the Bell, Watchman." We here copy the 3d stanza and its refrain :—

> Here's where the bright days of childhood's delight
> Passed with no care for the world's dreary night ;
> Here's where the dreams of our youth still remain :
> How we love to think of being home, home again.
>
> CHORUS.
> Join the song, sister — sing, brother, sing,
> Loud let your voices with thankfulness ring !
> Hark ! hear the echoes, they join the refrain —
> " Happy, happy are we, for we're home, home again."

We have seldom heard a piece better executed, than was this appropriate Ode, even by amateur musicians. The family also sang, in excellent time and manner, quite a number of popular Southern Ballads, all of which were accompanied on a melodeon by the wife of Jacob Irving Wendell, who seemed prepared to touch any keys requisite to their performance. It is a great pleasure to witness such a family gathering, but a saddening reflection to think that not even the youngest member assembled at such a joyous fireside, will be alive an hundred years hence.

> Let them assemble in harmony all,
> Just as by fiat of Death they may fall :
> The old and grown up, the young and the small ;
> Though forgotten by us in Time's sable pall ;
> For gathered they will be as God bids them rise
> To a Thanksgiving Supper prepared in the skies.

From the Canajoharie Radii.

OBITUARY.

BY J. R. SIMMS, ESQ., OF FORT PLAIN, N. Y.

We are grieved to know that death claims as its victim our young friend, Wellington C. Wendell, who died at his residence in Albany, on Friday night of last week, at the age of forty years. He was the eldest son of Jacob Wendell, Esq., of this village, at whose residence, as we told the readers of the *Radii* last week, he was a member of the family gathering on Thanksgiving Day of the week before. Starting life as a young man of promise, he learned the printer's trade of Levi S. Backus, the mute editor — a trade which rapidly cultivates the intellect of a reflecting mind. He was for a time engaged with C. W. Webster, Esq., in the publication of our village newspaper; and on disposing of his interest in the concern he removed to Albany. For several years he was there employed as a practical printer in the office of *The Evening Journal*. Subsequently he went to Philadelphia, to serve as book-keeper in the establishment of Howe's Sewing Machine Company. Returning to Albany, he became book-keeper in the Piano house of Marshall and Wendell, in which he was still engaged. That he had labored so long and faithfully, and not laid up a fortune of worldly treasure, is not to be attributed to a want either of ability or industry. Indeed, he invented the rubber slate, obviating a world of noise; but we are not aware that the patent was ever of much value to him. With good habits, good qualifications, suavity of manners, and industry, he failed to amass wealth — another striking exemplification of the fact that all are not born to be rich. His was a generous and confiding nature, and he was the most loved and respected by those to whom he was the best known.

On November 16th, he was attacked with the spinal or spotted fever. Under proper treatment he had so far recovered as to feel justified in being at the family gathering, at his paternal home in this place, on Thanksgiving Day. There were few happier families assembled on that occasion in the Mohawk Valley, (he making one of the number,) than was that of his father, Jacob Wendell, Esq. An Ode of no little merit, prepared for the occasion by this son, and entitled "*Home, Home, Again,*" we have already told your readers was sung with fine effect on Thanksgiving evening in our hearing, *his* voice swelling the melody to the close of the last stanza. He returned to Albany on Tuesday of last week, and early on Wednesday morning his disease manifested itself anew, by a violent pain in the back of the neck. He soon became unconscious, and with a few lucid intervals remained so until life's flickering lamp went out, at 12 o'clock on Friday night, when he fell into that slumber which man cannot disturb, and his spirit, freed from a tabernacle of flesh, and given a spiritual tabernacle, prepared by the Great Architect who never yet gave an illy-fitting one, went home as the first of the assembled family — to that Thanksgiving Supper prepared in the skies. Thus, by the wonder-working and mysterious hand of Creative Wisdom, has another social and useful man been cut down in his prime, and his friends and community left to mourn their sad bereavement. His funeral, which was largely attended, took place, at the residence of his brother, N. D. Wendell, Esq., 46 Chestnut street, on Monday P. M., where were assembled an unusual number of friends and heart-grieving mourners; the Rev. Mr. Hulburd, of the Hudson Street M. E. Church, assisted by the Rev. Homer Eaton, once a pastor of our village church, officiating.

God grant that the stricken widow and Miss Ida — her only child — may, with friendship's warmest sympathy, find HIM a sufficient support in this their hour of greatest need.

From the Albany Evening Journal.

DEATH OF W. C. WENDELL.

The death of Mr. W. C. Wendell, of this city, announced on Saturday, merits more than passing notice. Several years since he was connected with the Evening Journal book and job office, and since then he has filled various responsible positions of a business nature. At the time of his death he was book-keeper in the piano house of Marshall & Wendell. He was a son of Jacob Wendell, of Fort Plain, and brother of Nathan D. Wendell, the newly elected Albany County Treasurer and Cashier of the Merchants Bank. Mr. Wendell possessed innumerable graces of character, and in all the relations of life he invariably won the regard and esteem of those with whom he came in contact. His attachments to personal friends were characterized by much more than ordinary warmth and sincerity. His sudden death, in the prime of life, will be a sad blow to his sorrowing relatives, and will be deeply regretted by numerous friends and acquaintances, who will treasure the remembrance of his honest worth and genial disposition.

In Memoriam.

From the Albany Sunday Press.

WELLINGTON C. WENDELL.

The sudden demise of this well-known citizen, brother of Cashier N. D. Wendell, caused great regret among his numerous friends and acquaintances. He was suffering from irritable condition of spine and back, which gave rise to severe neuralgic pains, and appeared to have completely recovered. On Wednesday, a week ago, he went to Fort Plain to be present at a family gathering, and to which all members of the family had been invited by Mr. Wendell's father. The gathering was a very agreeable and pleasant one. On Tuesday last, Mr. W. C. Wendell returned to his home in this city. After his return, he had a relapse, but appeared to be doing well. On Friday night, however, he had an unexpected attack of apoplexy, and died a few hours after of apoplexy and congestion of the brain.

From the Albany Knickerbocker.

SUDDEN DEATH.

On Friday night last Mr. Wellington C. Wendell, brother of County Treasurer Wendell, died very suddenly. It appears that a few weeks ago he was suffering from an irritable condition of the spine and back, which gave rise to severe neuralgic pains. Under kind and skilful treatment he appeared to have recovered. The day preceding last Thanksgiving he visited his father's home at Fort Plain, to attend a family gathering about the festive board on Thanksgiving Day. Deceased, as well as all others who were present, had an enjoyable time, and on Tuesday last

Mr. W. C. Wendell returned to his home in this city. On his return he had a relapse, and on Friday night had an unexpected attack of apoplexy, and died in a few hours. Apoplexy and congestion of the brain were the immediate causes of death.

From the Albany Evening Times.

The Funeral of Mr. Wendell.

The funeral of the late W. C. Wendell took place, this afternoon, from the residence of his brother, Mr. N. D. Wendell, No. 46 Chestnut street, and was very largely attended by the relatives and the numerous friends of the deceased. Mr. Wendell's death was rather unexpected, it being believed that he had nearly recovered from his recent indisposition which had confined him to his room for some time. On Thanksgiving Day he had assembled with other members of the family at the old homestead in Montgomery county, and his kindly face was bright and joyous at the gathering again of those who came together in such goodly numbers. Upon his return home he was again taken ill, yet it was supposed the sickness was not dangerous; and all were surprised to hear that grim Death had laid his cold hand on this genial gentleman.

Mr. Wendell was widely known and as widely esteemed; his good qualities were many, and his disposition warm and generous; he possessed the business integrity and steadiness characteristic of the Wendell family, and his death will be sincerely mourned by all with whom he ever came in contact.

Contents.

I. MISCELLANEOUS POEMS:

Mother,	1
To day I'm thirty-two,	4
To Lizzie,	6
To Sister Luthera,	7
To Libbie,	7
To Sister Aurelia,	8
To Little Ida,	9
To Margaret,	10
To Lillie,	11
To Libbie,	11
For a Friend,	11
To Dora and Alice B.,	12
To ——— " ———,	13
To A Friend, (two),	14
To A Friend, (two),	15
No charms without Thee,	16
Never Forgotten,	17
Friendship,	18
Jennie,	18
Do not forget,	19
Think of me yet,	20
Golden Chain,	21
I choose to be alone,	22
Think of me Frank,	22
Hoping,	23
Wishing,	24
To Mollie,	25

I. Miscellaneous Poems:

Awaiting Thanksgiving,	25
Home, Home Again,	26
My absent Sister,	28
Days of Youth,	29
His return,	29
Christmas Carol,	30
A Thought for you,	32
To ——,	32
Christmas Hymn,	33
Sweet Bye and Bye,	34
Welcome at the Door,	35
Speak gentle words,	36
Naked Truth,	37
Singing from the heart,	38
Light,	38
Spring Time,	39
Absent,	40
Searching for the Sea,	42
On a Lock of Hair,	44
Brooklet,	44
At Rest,	45
Nothing Lost,	45
On the death of Mrs. Jane Clover,	47
On the death of Jessie Tompkins,	48
Jessie Asleep,	49
Lines written in a Bible, etc.,	49
Only asleep,	50
Our Gem above,	51
Little Mary Ann Carroll,	51
On the death of Miss Ida Keyes,	52
Ma, never told a lie,	53
The Chime,	55
A year ago to-day,	56
For an Album,	58
Friendship,	59
A mother's gift,	59
A Prayer,	60

II. HUMOROUS:

Comfort, By Kate B. T.,	61
Reply to Kate B. T.	62
To Sister Luthera,	64
To Sister Aurelia,	66
To Charles Wendell,	68
Keep Pace with the Times,	71
I'd Rather,	73
Bachelor's Hall,	74
A Bachelor,	76
A Lesson from the Glass Steam Engine,	77
Conquest of the Conqueror,	79
It's the fashion, Don't you Know?	82
The Dollar mark,	84
Montowese Narrows,	85
Coney Island,	88
For the fun of the thing,	90
The Power of Example,	91
The Yankee Pass,	94
Offer of John Bull to Miss Columbia,	98
Reply of Miss Columbia to John Bull,	100
Acrostic,	102
Old Pat is Dead,	102

III. PATRIOTIC:

The Soldier's Good Bye,	104
The Dying Volunteer,	106
To Capt. Nelson O. Wendell,	108
Freedom's Gift,	110
What the Boys in blue say,	113
The Northern Peace Makers,	116
Welcome Peace,	118
The Return of Peace,	119
Kansas and Freedom,	120
To the XLth Congress,	122

IV. POLITICAL:

    Match him, ... 123
    Marching Along, ... 126
    When Grant goes marching in, ... 127
    Glory Hallelujah, ... 129
    Grant and the Union, ... 130
    Marching Along, ... 132

V. ADDRESSES:

    We greet you, ... 133
    Second Part. 134
    Carrier's Annual greeting, , ... 137
    Second Annual Address, ... 148

VI. APPENDIX, IN MEMORIAM:

    Capt. Nelson O. Wendell, ... 151

POEMS:

MISCELLANEOUS, HUMOROUS, PATRIOTIC,
AND POLITICAL.

I. MISCELLANEOUS.

MOTHER.

I'm sitting quite alone, Mother,
   All else of busy life
Were wooed and won some hours since
   By sleep, from daily strife;
But Morpheus, with his luring smile,
   Has not a charm for me —
My mind is occupied the while
   With thoughts of home and thee, Mother,
   With thoughts of home and thee.

I thank the God of light, Mother,
   For mem'ry's lamp, to peer
What, else, would dim the retrospect
   Of our sojourning here;

For, by the lurid ray that gleams
    Across the mystic main,
My thoughts revert, and then it seems
    That I am young again, Mother,
    That I am young again.

I hear your gentle voice, Mother,
    In earnest tones entreat
That sin might never chill my heart
    Or gyve my tender feet;
How well my life has answer'd those
    Maternal prayers of thine,
I leave to God, who, only, knows
    What's in this heart of mine, Mother,
    What's in this heart of mine.

My lips so love to dwell, Mother,
    Upon that hallowed word,
Whose music makes the fondest chord
    Of heart-emotions, stirred,
That I am loth to hear anew
    The notes of matin bell,
That call my thoughts away from you,
    On whom they love to dwell, Mother,
    On whom they love to dwell.

About thy holy name, Mother,
   My richest feelings close
In fond embrace, that mocks to shame
   The fire that passion knows;
Whate'er I do, where'er I rove,
   Thy name is ever near —
O, 'tis the bliss of life to love
   A name so full of cheer, Mother,
   A name so full of cheer.

The busy hand of time, Mother,
   Has left the telling trace
Of silver threads upon your head,
   And age upon your face;
Yet, though he strike our hands apart,
   And bear you from my sight,
You still shall occupy my heart
   As fully as to-night, Mother,
   As fully as to-night.

MISCELLANEOUS POEMS.

THIRTY-TWO.

[Jan. 30, 1864.]

To-day I'm walking in the paths
   Of Mem'ry's blest retreat:
To-day the Present and the Past
   In full fruition meet.
In spirit-rambling through the shades,
   Now fresh as morning dew,
I dream that I am young again, —
   I *know* I'm thirty-two.

I stand beside the stream, that rolls
   'Tween youth and riper years;
I gaze upon the other shore,
   Unfraught with worldly fears;
Then glance adown the slope of life,
   That future holds in view,
And meditate, in earnest thought,
   "To-day I'm thirty-two."

Here stands a vow that I have made;
   There lies a broken pledge;
While just beyond lie buoyant hopes
   Wrecked on misfortune's ledge:

Yet happy hours bedeck the sky,
    And let their glories through,
And seem to join with me in joy, —
    To-day I'm thirty-two.

Here winds the path that friends have trod —
    Its terminus is love, —
Some found the goal with me, and some
    Are registered above.
The rose of fond remembrance blooms
    In colors ever new,
And calls me back to other days,
    From thoughts of " thirty-two."

'Twas here, imagination's loom
    Was reared upon the sand,
And warp and woof found comely form,
    Beneath my plastic hand.
But ah! the future proved my web
    But gossamer and dew, —
I've lived to see them all dissolve,
    From youth to thirty-two.

Behind me masks of mirth, and cloaks,
    Whose mission seemed to be
To place me in another sphere
    Than God designed for me —

Are mocking monuments, to-day,
    Of what I used to do
Before I turned that point of life,
    That brought me thirty-two.

Long since the domes and minarets
    Of castles in the air,
Have gathered folly's moss about
    Their ruins lying there.
I ramble 'mid the gloomy waste,
    And pledge my vow anew,
To build on Caution's corner-stone,
    Henceforth, from thirty-two.

LIZZIE.[1]

With eyes filled with tears — with hearts overflowing —
    We have watched Lizzie's journey through sorrow and pain.
While we mourn, there is sweet consolation in knowing,
    She is only asleep — we shall see her again.

---

[1] Wife of Harvey Wendell, who died June 28, 1861.

TO SISTER LUTHERA.

Just before the morning breaks,
   Nature wears its darkest frown,
Dons the sable cloak, and makes
   Dismal, every thing around.

But the cheering rays of light,
   Come at matin's blessed hour,
Clothe in garments pleasing, bright
   Nature, by its magic power.

Sister! so throughout our days
   Darkest clouds of sorrow pass,
Just before the promised rays
   Bring us joy and happiness.

TO LIBBIE.

Life would seem a dreary ocean,
Isleless, with no port to gain,
But for friendship's star, Devotion,
Brightening the mystic main.
In thy journey o'er the sea
Ever may it beam on thee.

Miscellaneous Poems.

TO SISTER AURELIA

ON THE BIRTH OF HER FIRST-BORN CHILD.

Sweet recompense! Hope gemmed the night,
   While Patience kept away Despair;
Fruition gave to home a light —
   Love left an angel there.

Parental bliss! O who can mete
   But God, a mother's holy love!
Who prove a father's bliss complete
   But Father up above!

Completing link! Two hearts are bound
   In closer unison by thee —
A firmer chain is thrown around
   Our weak humanity.

O! blessed trust! Two little feet,
   To trudge the way to Him who gave;
Another heart to keep complete,
   Another soul to save.

Feb. 12th, 1865.

LITTLE IDA.[1]

Just as coming morn is weaving
   Bars of gold o'er hill and plain,
And in buried glory leaving
   Luna and her twinkling train,

Little eyes are sweetly peering
   Out from 'neath the coverlid,
Laden, with the most endearing
   Smiles, that ever dimples hid.

From the time of morning's waking,
   To the paling of the day,
Little voice and feet are taking
   All the liberties of play;

Castle-building, thoughts are teeming, —
   Not a care to check her glee, —
Seems the earnest of the dreaming,
   Clothed in pure simplicity.

---
[1] The author's only child.

Innocence and mirth inviting,
    Scenes that babyhood imparts,
Serve as torches in the lighting
    Happy home, and happy hearts.

With the past, inurned will slumber
    Soon, the sweetest time of life;
Soon will cares, in ceaseless number,
    Call her to the rugged strife.

Little Ida! may thy morrow,
    Like thy babyhood's to-day,
Know but little of the sorrow
    Life has scattered o'er the way.

TO MARGARET.

Moss shall never girt the fountain,
At which friendship holds the cup,
Rilling from the holy mountain,
God for love hath towered up.
At its fount I'll quaff devotion,
Round thy name forever more,
Even as the sands of ocean
Toss, unceasing, on the shore.

LILLIE.

Like the bow which spans the heaven,
In the arch of blue,
Lifts the hopes, and like the leaven
Lightens promise too, —
Is thy smile, and may its rays
Early light some mortal's days.

TO LIBBIE.

Life, like the ocean, has gems that are hidden
In its safe bosom, the world cannot see —
Blessed be friendship! with it I am bidden
Bring to the surface the value in thee.
Imaging *worth, admiration* and *love* —
Each one a crown in the glory above.

FOR A FRIEND.

As down in the sunless retreats of the ocean
Sweet flowers are blooming no mortal can see,
So deep in my bosom is friendship's devotion,
Unseen by the world, still remembering thee.

TO DORA AND ALICE B.

My dear little nieces — both Dora and Alice —
   Say, why don't you write me a letter or two?
I am sure that it cannot be hatred or malice
   That keeps me from getting a letter from you.

Why don't you invite me to come out to Sherman,
   To join you in romping and having such fun?
You don't know but that I might quickly determine
   To take up the offer and travel from home.

I think that I'd like, with my two little nieces,
   To hunt for some eggs, in the barn or the mow,
Or drive down to water the chicks and the geeses,
   Or ride into market astraddle the cow.

Now, won't you please write me a nice little letter,
   Just to show that you sometimes are thinking of me?
In directing the envelope I think you had better
   Say — "Albany, Eagle street, one sixty-three."

T O ———

Oh ! heart, be still ! stop pulsing for a love
   Whose ripened sheaf dare not be garnered here,
Stop ! let the past as registered above
   Find not a grave within a single tear.

The gyve is strong ! Its chafing wears the span
   In fruitless efforts looking for release.
Break ! ere my soul evokes a frenzied ban
   On home and hope, pure happiness and peace.

The chalice tempts ! Oh ! take it from my sight ;
   'Twere better that my heart should go athirst
Than know each drop I drink of its delight
   But sinks my soul much deeper than the first.

My prayers for thee ! Give back my empty hand ;
   I'll battle with the cares of coming years ;
And anchor hope that in the happy land
   We'll know and love, without regret or tears.

TO A FRIEND.

They tell me thou art gay
In thy palace far away
Where another reaps the smile that once was
    mine, my love,
And my heart is sad and low
For I think of long ago
And the folly of this heart that once was thine, my
    love.

TO A FRIEND.

In my unbroken chain of affection,
    That is formed of the tried and the true,
One gem of the circle collection
    Is the link emblematic of you.

May no act of the future dissever
    That circle that binds you to me;
No rust of forgetfulness ever
    Destroy my remembrance of thee.

TO A FRIEND.

The dew of morning ne'er forgets
    To fill the waiting lily's cup;
Nor morning sun to bend its rays,
    And pick the jewel up.

The twinkling stars that fleck the dome
    When evening drops its sable robe,
Remember well their path to roam
    About our little globe.

As constant may I hope to find
    The cup of friendship held by thee;
And trust that in the fading years
    You'll still remember me.

NO CHARMS WITHOUT THEE.

Life hath lost its charms without thee;
(Heaven throw a shield about thee!)
Thoughts but mock the passing hours, waiting
for the coming day.
Sleep refuses aid for dreaming
Only sorrow thoughts are streaming
Through my aching brain, while thinking of my
darling far away.

Could the promised sun to-morrow
Wake me from this brooding sorrow —
Could it find the chalice broken whence I quaff
so much of grief —
Hope would span anew the heaven
Which by gloomy thought is riven,
And anew my soul would ramble in the garden
of relief.

NEVER FORGOTTEN.

Within the domain of pure love and affection,
   Encircled by dreams of the present and past,
Lives a friend, whom I cherish in fond recollection
   Let it ever be so, while the future shall last.

Yes, the storms of affliction and sorrow encumber
   The mariner over life's turbulent sea;
O! that I might be one, who could lessen the number,
   Kind friend, — of the storms that are waiting for thee.

In your labor of weaving the web of devotion,
   Turn a thought on the one who will never forget;
Thus assuring a friend — though on life's changeful ocean,
   You have never forgotten — but think of me yet.

FRIENDSHIP—JENNIE.

Jewel in the rich tiara,
Emerald of brightest sheen:
Naught but Death's unknown Sahara
Ne'er shall dim its light serene.
Iris to the soul — its rays
Ever point to happy days.

TO ——

This humble tribute please receive
   With earnest wishes from the heart
Of each the donors, who believe
   True friendship but a noble art.

Upon our mem'ry's choicest page
   Is graven like a magic charm
Thy name, which neither rust nor age,
   Nor cold neglect, shall bring to harm.

DO NOT FORGET.

Do not forget me, dear,
   Do not forget;
Earnest I'm praying, dear,
   Loving thee yet;
Cherish the promises
   Vow'd when we met,
Do not forget me, dear,
   Do not forget.

Join with the gaily, dear,
   Seek to alloy
Sadness with happiness,
   Sorrow with joy:
I would not deprive thee
   Such happiness, yet
Do not forget me, dear,
   Do not forget.

Wander in sunny climes,
   Over the sea;
Clamber the Appenines,
   Happy and free;

Banish the sorrowful,
    Bury regret——
Do not forget me, dear,
    Do not forget.

Go where soft breezes, love,
    Rock thee to sleep;
List to the music, love,
    Fairy-like sweep
Over sweet Italy
    Freely, and yet
Do not forget me, dear,
    Do not forget.

Faith in thy promises
    Lightens my heart,
Pictures thy image, dear,
    Just as thou art;
Remember, in earnest
    I'm loving thee yet —
Do not forget me, dear,
    Do not forget.

THINK OF ME YET.

Friends of the years long ago,
   Pictures I cannot forget,
Oh! it were pleasant to know
   Some of them think of me yet.
Would that my wishes could fly
   Safe o'er the sea and the foam,
Some one would read in my sigh
   A wish for a letter from home.

GOLDEN CHAIN.

As the dew that is kissed by the sun on the flower
   Enlivens and fills it with sweetness and breath,
So I trust that the chain that is woven this hour
   May unite us in friendship 'till severed by death.

I CHOOSE TO BE ALONE.

A wild, wet night! The driving sleet
   Blurs all the lamps along the quay;
The windows shake; the busy street
Is yet alive with hurrying feet;
   The wind raves from the sea.

So let it rave! My lamp burns bright;
   My long day's work is almost done;
I curtain out each sound and sight—
Of all nights in the year, to-night
   I choose to be alone.

THINK OF ME, FRANK.

Friendship, true, will never die;
Reason shows the reason why;
And where'er you find a rest —
North, or South, or East, or West —
Kindly think of me.

HOPING.

Stealing through my lattice window
    Comes the sun,
Heralding another morning,
    Just begun,
Every ray replete with blessing,
Rich and poor alike caressing,
And with welcome glee addressing
    Every one.

Darling Willie, I am hoping
    Bye and bye,
When this wicked war is over,
    You and I,
By the pledges we have plighted,
    In the heart of home delighted
Shall again be re-united
    'Till we die.

WISHES.

That I were but a poet,
That I'd the power to show it
That all the world should know it,
    My darling, O, my darling.

I'd give interpretation
To ev'ry exclamation,
And take you on probation,
    My darling, O, my darling.

"That life were but beginning,"
(A baby — sure as sinning —
If so, you'd be more winning)
    My darling, O, my darling.

"That memory were not grievous" —
(If you've been naughty, leave us,
Don't *wish*, and then deceive us,)
    My darling, O, my darling.

"That loving were not sinning,"
(It never is when "winning"
Adheres to the beginning,)
    My darling, O, my darling.

AWAITING THANKSGIVING.

Three days yet of tugging and toiling and strife,
When I, with my " little one," baggage and wife,
Will set out on a journey, nor tarry until
We arrive at the cottage just under the hill.[1]

And while I am writing my fancy is fed,
And visions of *eatables* dance through my head.
O, hasten the gala-day! When will it come?
I'm *so* tired of waiting, and want to go home.

    Nov. 23, 1862.

TO MOLLIE.

Many a gem's in the depths of the ocean,
Over which waves may unceasingly roll.
Like unto it is the gem of devotion
  Living, though seeming asleep, in the soul;
Imaging only its welcoming light,
  Earnest to him who is blessed with the right.

---

[1] Referring to the old homestead, the residence of his parents at Fort Plain.

HOME, HOME AGAIN.

THANKSGIVING DAY.

Air.—"*Ring the Bell, Watchman.*"

Long, long the days of thy coming appeared,
Blest day, by sweet recollections endeared;
But from the valley, the hill and the plain,
Thanksgiving Day has brought us home, home
    again.

Chorus.

Join the song, sister — sing, brother, sing,
Loud let your voices with thankfulness ring!
Hark! hear the echoes, they join the refrain —
"Happy, happy are we, for we're home, home
    again."

Spring-time has gathered its richest perfume,
Summer has reaped from the blossom and bloom,
Autumn has garnered the fruit and the grain,
Winter comes, and we are gathered home, home
    again.

Here's where the bright days of childhood's delight,
Passed with no care for the world's dreary night;
Here's where the dreams of our youth still remain :
How we love to think of being home, home again.

Still we've the hand of a Father to bless;
Still we've a kind Mother's smile and caress;
Still we've a welcome that's worthy the name;
O! how much of joy we find in " home, home again."

Yes, yes, the good time, so joyous and gay,
Ever remember'd, is with us to-day;
Raise, raise your voices, and spread the refrain —
Union forevermore! we're home, home again.

FORT PLAIN, N. Y., December 7, 1865,
        November 28, 1872.

MY ABSENT SISTER.[1]

THANKSGIVING DAY.

The only thought that mars
    Our festive joys to-day,
Is, that our circle's not complete,
    One sister is away.

But in our thanks we'll not forget
    You still are in the chain;
And in our hearts we hope and pray
    We yet may meet again.

Nov. 28, 1872.

---

[1] The author's last written production, embodied in a family letter sent to his sister, Mrs. H. L. Harter, of Potsdam, N. Y.

DAYS OF YOUTH.

O! days of youth! In retrospect I turn thy pages o'er,
And read them with a zest that I have never felt before;
I feel that all my "active life" is sluggish in its flow
Compared with Youth's bright rivulet of twenty years ago.

HIS RETURN.

I came here a stranger, I thought 'twould be joy
In my manhood to roam where I roamed when a boy, —
I have learned that deep sorrow a day may impart,
With the shadow of graves hanging over the heart.

CHRISTMAS CAROL.

I.

Gladly the bells are ringing,
    Sing merry Christmas,
    Sing merry Christmas,
Hope in the heart is springing,
    Christ is with us to-day.

Chorus.

Ring the bells,
Ring the bells for the merry, merry, merry, merry Christmas,
Ring the bells,
Ring the bells for the merry, merry, merry, merry Christmas.

II.

Brightly the star is nearing,
    Sing merry Christmas,
    Sing merry Christmas,
Jesus the Christ appearing,
    Lowly in Bethlehem.

III.

Light up your hearts with gladness,
 Sing merry Christmas,
 Sing merry Christmas,
Out from the clouds of sadness
 Jesus, our Hope, appears.

IV.

Sing we the same glad story,
 Sing merry Christmas,
 Sing merry Christmas,
There is a crown of glory,
 Waiting for you and me.

The *Albany Evening Journal* of Dec. 14, 1872, in referring to the foregoing, says: — "The music, which is by our townsman, Mr. Theo. Mosher, is arranged for soprano, alto and bass, trio and chorus, and while within the capacity of most musicians, it possesses an artistic merit not always found in Christmas music. In its unaffected simplicity and appropriateness to the occasion, as well as its spirited and graceful movement, it constitutes a real gem. The words of the carol, which, we may observe, were written by the late W. C. Wendell, whose death was announced but a few days ago, breathe throughout a joyous, hopeful spirit, and are well adapted to the music which is wedded to them."

A THOUGHT FOR YOU.

When moods of low despondency like curtains hide the light,
And bring me only shadows that foretell the coming night,
Or when a ray of hope escapes from out the heavy blue
To cheer my heart — at either time, I have a thought for you.

TO ———

Darkness is on the hearth,
Naught do I say,
Books are but little worth;
Thou art away.
Voices, the true and kind,
Strange are to me,
I have lost heart and mind
Thinking of thee.

CHRISTMAS HYMN.

Sung at South Dutch Church Sunday School Anniversary,
at Albany.

[Dec. 25, 1856.]

Away! away! away we go,
   Merrily o'er the fleecy snow,
Away! away! away we go,
   Merrily on we go.
Roses bloom where dimples play
   On the cheek of mirth,
Sweetly chasing care away
   O'er the shrouded earth.

Away! away! away we go,
   Merrily o'er the fleecy snow,
Away! away! away we go,
   Merrily on we go.
Happy let our voices sing
   At this jubilee,
Dearest gems of mem'ry cling,
   Sabbath School, to thee.

SWEET BYE AND BYE.

[When the popular air, "Sweet Bye and Bye," was first published, having but three stanzas, the following two were added by the author.]

We have friends on that beautiful shore,
   Who are waiting to meet us with glee,
Where " Good Bye" will be said nevermore,
   While the Saviour in glory we see.
     CHORUS.— " In the Sweet Bye and Bye," &c.

There is peace on that beautiful shore,
   There is rest for the weary above,
There with Jesus we'll rest ever more,
   And partake of his bountiful love.
     CHORUS.— " In the Sweet Bye and Bye," &c.

WINTER COMES AGAIN.

Spring-time ne'er forgets its roses —
   Summer's sun its ripening grain,
Autumn in its wealth reposes,
   Winter comes again.

WELCOME AT THE DOOR.

While the years of Time roll o'er us,
    While care and sorrow go before,
Still we'll sing our happy chorus —
    " We've friends to welcome at the door."
There is pleasure in the meeting
    When absence makes you love the more,
When the hand and heart are greeting
    The friends we welcome at the door.

    Long may it be Heaven's pleasure —
        Long this blessing keep in store —
    Long to cherish it a treasure,
        Meeting loved ones at the door.

Here the sister meets with brother,
    Long parted from the olden shore;
Here a father, here a mother,
    All meet to welcome at the door.
Mem'ries rise and pass before us
    Of those we loved but see no more,
But they sing the Heavenly chorus,
    And bid us welcome at the door.

SPEAK GENTLE WORDS.

Speak gentle words! The lip may edge
    The poorest gift with welcome gold!
May drop pure seed among the sedge,
    Whose yield may be "a thousand fold."

Speak gentle words! Perchance some breast
    By guilt inflamed, may drink them in,
And from their soothing find a rest
    Beyond the baleful reach of sin.

Speak gentle words! The little child
    Bereft, and cast upon the stage,
Might mutely bless, and when she smiled,
    Light up with thanks her orphanage.

Speak gentle words! Their mystic charm
    A Saviour won to you and me!
They often shield a soul from harm
    And save one for eternity.

"NAKED" TRUTH.

Truth and Falsehood once together
   Chanced to meet, and in the path
Both agreed the sultry weather
   Bid them take a river bath.

So, disrobing, quick disported
   They within the cooling tide;
Found the balm that each had courted
   Ev'ry wish had satisfied.

Falsehood, being first at leaving,
   Clothed himself with Truth's array,
Took the good clothes — Truth deceiving —
   Left his rags and sped away.

Truth disdains the lie to practice —
   Falsehood travels like a prince —
Dating from the bath, the fact is
   Truth's been *naked* ever since.

June 26, 1869.

LIGHT.

[Oct. 29, 1863.]

Light, in silver rays descending,
    Starts the lily from her rest,
Leaves a wake of joy and gladness
    In her journey to the west.

Light, impartial, bathes in splendor
    Lowly roof and palace dome,
Streaming in the lordly mansion,
    Gladdening the cottage home.

SINGING FROM THE HEART.

If you have a pleasant thought — sing it, sing it —
Like the birdies in their sport, sing it from the heart.
    Does the Holy Spirit move
    For the lambkins of His love,
Sing and point the fold above, sing it from the heart.

Are you weary, are you sad — sing it, sing it —
Make yourselves and others glad — sing it from
  the heart.
  Angels up before His face
  Sing of His redeeming grace,
Give the Saviour endless praise — sing it from the
  heart.

Ev'ry gracious deed of His — sing it, sing it,
Nothing sounds so well as this — sing it from the
  heart.
  How He walked upon the wave
  Rescued Lazarus from the grave,
Died our guilty souls to save — sing it from the
  heart.

SPRING-TIME.

The beauties of Spring-time — its sunshine and
  showers,
Its birds, buds and blossoms, and beautiful
  flowers,
Have received the attention of poets and sages
From Ossian down through the cycle of ages.

ABSENT.

Spring has spoken to the flowers,
 Through the sunbeams and the showers;
Blossoms cast their fragrance freely, as they
 did in days of yore;
 Still the work of Nature's fingers,
 And the warble of her singers
Do not have the winning power, that they always
 had before.

Life has lost its charms without thee —
 (Heaven keep its shield about thee) —
Thoughts but mock the passing hours, waiting
 for the coming day;
 Sleep refuses aid for dreaming —
 Only sorrow-thoughts are streaming
Through my aching brain, while thinking of my
 darling, far away.

Could the promised sun to-morrow
Wake me from this brooding sorrow;

Could it find the chalice broken, whence
    I quaff so much of grief, —
  Hope would span anew the heaven
  Which by gloomy thought is riven,
And afresh my soul would ramble in the garden
    of relief.

  Though I walk in happy places —
  Though I see familiar faces —
Though their sympathetic voices tell of friend-
    ship unalloyed ;
  Still there is a shade and sorrow
  Shrouds the vision of to-morrow,
There's no other but thee, darling, that can
    fill the aching void.

  But I feel the time is nearing,
  When, these war-clouds disappearing,
Peace, shall ring from every lyre — Union be
    the glad refrain ;
  Then, united, we will ever
  Send petitions to the Giver,
That the curse of war may never cloud
    our happy home again.

    Albany May 29, 1863.

SEARCHING FOR THE SEA.

From out a fissure in the rock, against the
  rugged hill,
Came trickling at my feet the drops that
  formed a little rill :
The rill in creeping down the slope — so like a
  silver thread —
Seemed whispering with infant glee, and
  this is what it said :
  "I'm free and happy, yet I will
   That I should happier be ;
  I shall not always be a rill —
   I'm searching for the sea."

The little brook, in merry glee, came dancing
  through the dell,
And sang a happy song for me as o'er the
  rocks it fell ;
Then tripped away, with music sweet, adown
  its pebble bed —
My ear was charmed, I list'ning stood, and
  this is what it said :

"I'm free and happy, but I dream
   That I shall happier be;
I shall not always be a stream —
   I'm searching for the sea."

I stood upon the mossy bank, just by the
         river's side,
And watched, as wave was crowding wave
         adown the mighty tide;
While from a thousand little tongues from
         out that crystal head
Came words that cheered my drooping heart,
         and this is what they said:
   "We're free and happy, yet we hope
      That we may happier be;
   We're looking for a wider scope —
      We're searching for the sea."

Each mortal has a course to run: the babe
         at mother's breast;
The child just stepping in the world to
         battle with the rest;
The middle-aged whose life has passed
         from rill and brook to river —
All journey on to meet the sea that finds
         no shores forever.

While in the current flow of years,
   Each heart may happier be,
By keeping smiles above the tears
   In searching for the sea.

Albany, Dec. 21, 1865.

ON A LOCK OF HAIR.

O, little waif, how memory's light
   Illumes the past at sight of thee;
I'll treasure, with a fond delight,
   The pleasant dreams you bring to me.

BROOKLET.

Dancing lightly through the meadow —
   Bounding gladly o'er the lea,
Now in sunlight, now in shadow —
   Searching for the sea,
Wends the little brooklet, making
   Music for its tripping feet,
Mindless of the troubled quaking
   Other objects meet.

AT REST.

At rest! how consoling the thought that the morrow—
Laden ever with trouble, vexation and pain—
Shall forever pass by with its burden of sorrow,
And never disturb our Mother again.

NOTHING LOST.

[Sep. 20, 1860.]

Each pearly drop of dew that rolls
    From evening's curtained crest,
And seeks within the lily's folds
    A biding place and rest,
Is sought by morning's coming gleam
    That dazzles o'er the plain,
And by the fingers of its sheen
    Is taken home again.

Each wholesome thought that springs to light
   From its sojourning place,
Commissioned in its errand-flight
   To benefit the race,
May mutely speed—like snowy flake
   Fall gently on the lea,
Yet with an arm of power shake
   Debased humanity.

Each act of love that singles out
   A follower of sin,
And sallies on the strong redoubt
   Determining to win,
May sunder many a tilting lance
   While fraying with the foe,
Yet finally they will advance
   With kisses for the blow.

Each word that consolation pours
   In sorrow's aching heart,
And points to beatific shores
   Where friends shall never part;
Will glide aloft on plumed wings
   And gather with the weight
Of goodly deeds that welcome brings
   In that eternal state.

LINES.

On the death of Jane, wife of Edward Clover, who died July 7, 1865.

Asleep in peace! The hush of death
   Surrounds her earthly bed to-night;
Still is the voice, and gone the breath:
But Mother *lives* with him who saith
   "I am the way and light."

We weep and grieve! We never knew,
   'Till Death unsealed the fount of tears,
How much we loved, nor yet how few
The hours left for us to do
   Full homage to her years.

The star of Faith! Its cheering rays
   Was Mother's compass o'er the sea;
Its light repelled the doubting haze,
Illuminating the darkest days,
   Before the soul was free.

Asleep in peace! The wildest blast
  Shall harmless pass her resting place:
The voyage o'er, her anchor's cast
Within the haven where at last
  We hope to see her face.

LINES

On the death of Jessie, only daughter of James and Sarah Tompkins, aged 2 years, 4 months, and 2 days.

Out from sorrow 'till the morrow,
  One too pure for earth to own;
Passed the portal of the mortal,
  Waits the father's welcome home.

She is sleeping — we are weeping —
  She in peace, and we in pain;
But, O Father, by thy keeping,
  We shall see her wake again.

LINES

Written in a Bible presented to C. H. — N. Y. S. Militia, 25th Regiment, previous to his departure for Washington.

May the blessings of Heaven in showers
    descend,
And nerve you to follow our country's
    behest,
Encompass and guard, 'till the battle
    shall end,
And peace be restored, and the Nation
    at rest.

JESSIE ASLEEP.

Two summers' suns have waxed and waned
    Since erst was ushered into life —
Since first we dreamed our treasure gained,
    When Jessie entered in the strife.
    We met no ill to cause a sigh,
        No call for tears to weep,
    As mother sang the lullaby
        While Jessie went to sleep.

Parental love had done its part
  In welding hope within a chain
To bind to us the little heart,
  'Till He should take it home again.
    We little dreamed that Death was nigh,
      Our little sheaf to reap,
    While mother sang the lullaby
      As Jessie went to sleep.

Two simple years of test were given,
  By Father; then, His love to show,
He took the jewel up to heaven,
  And left the casket mould below.
    No weight of love beneath the sky
      Could our treasure keep;
    So angels sang the lullaby,
      And Jessie went to sleep.

ONLY ASLEEP.

Gone from the scenes of her sorrow and pain,
Gone from a land where the sorrowing weep,
Gone — but we know we shall see her again,
Blessed assurance — she is only asleep.

OUR GEM ABOVE.

Lines suggested by the death of Mary Ann, only daughter of James H. and Jane R. Carroll, who Died on Friday, February 27th, 1863 — in the fifth year of her age.

Just one week ago we owned
    A little gem —
Purer far than ever throned
    A diadem:
With a richer light it's glowing,
'Midst its kindred jewels growing,
And a Father's love is flowing
    Over them.

Like a lily, she was given
    For an hour —
But a bud to us, in Heaven
    Blooms the flower.
We had hoped the promised sweetness
Would mature to life's completeness;
But a higher life's repleteness
    Is her dower.

LINES

On the death of Ida Keyes, aged 11 years, and 5 months.

So sweet in life — a happy death
    Left tears for us — to Ida, rest.
Her little voice and latest breath,
    Proved that she loved the Saviour best.

O! happy thought — the morning light,
    That paled when our Ida died,
Will brighter grow — without a night —
    With angels on the sunny side.

Her little prayers, that we might meet
    Each other in the streets above,
Shall move our faith, for, O! 'tis sweet
    To think of meeting those we love.

"MA NEVER TOLD A LIE."

While passing through the busy street
   One drear December day,
A stranger saw two little feet
   Too cold to run or play.
Compassion for the boy quick led
   The stranger to his side —
"Pa, ma, and brother Willy's dead,
   And I am sick," he cried.

"I'm waiting, sir, for God to come —
   I've waited all the day;
I have no pa, no ma, no home,
   Nor where my head to lay.
But, sir, I know that God will see
   And hear me when I cry,
For ma said God would care for me —
   Ma never told a lie."

"Now, should you meet with God, please say
   That Benny's sick and cold,
And that he's waited all the day
   To gather in His fold.

Yet, O! it seems so long to be
   Without a home — I cry,
But ma said God would care for me —
   Ma never told a lie."

"God sent *me*, boy" — the stranger's voice
   Crept through the orphan's ear,
And made the little heart rejoice
   That God was found so near.
"God sent me here that I, my lad,
   Might give you better care,
Rewarding one in youth who had
   Faith in a mother's prayer."

"O! sir, a thousand thanks I owe —
   How shall I ever pay?
But how did God so quickly know
   Just where poor Benny lay?
Yet I was sure that God would see
   That Benny didn't die;
For ma said He would care for me —
   Ma never told a lie."

THE CHIME.

There is beauty and wonder in the flash
    and the thunder —
There's a melody sweet in the patter of rain;
There's a charm in the pages of Nature, though
    ages
  Have seen and perused them again and again.

There's a sweet source of pleasure — the featherly
    treasure,
  Perched safe in its cage — hear the notes, how
    they ring;
Not a care or a sorrow, not a dread of to-morrow!
  Ever happy! we envy the dear little thing.

There's accord in the fountain; in the rill from
    the mountain;
  In the murmuring brook and the dashing
    cascade;
.There are notes in the whistle that scatters the
    thistle
  When the wild wind is frolicking over the glade.

A YEAR AGO TO-DAY.

[Jan. 1, 1870.]

Now that we've passed the mystic line
   Between the Old and New,
We'll leave the new year for a time
   And '70 review.
A thousand little thoughts will come
   And found an active play,
By turning leaves and dating from
   A year ago to-day.

The records of a single year
   Are strangely interwrought
With life and death, with hope and fear,
   With gay and gloomy thought.
And few can turn the pages o'er,
   With truthfulness, and say,
"I've many friends, and had no more
   A year ago to-day."

Not many eyes, that now behold
    The dawning of the year,
Have not been witnesses that told
    The story of a tear!
Not many hearts, but what can claim
    Companionship with clay
That held a soul within its frame
    A year ago to-day.

How many, who essayed to climb
    Ambition's giddy mount,
Have fallen in this little time,
    None will attempt to count;
Yet Power, Gold and Lucifer
    Can shout aloud and say,
"As many follow as there were
    A year ago to-day."

FOR AN ALBUM.

Buds foretell the coming roses,
    Golden grain, the reaper's tread;
Little rain-drop presupposes
    Showers overhead.

Little waifs from Friendship's ocean,
    Harbored in this little book,
Speak a holier devotion
    Than a word or look.

Go thou forth upon thy mission,
    Gather every precious gem;
Friendship then will be fruition —
    Love, my diadem.

FRIENDSHIP.

True friendship ever will reflect
   Its picture on the yielding heart,
And only fade when cold neglect
   Strikes friendly hands apart.

Like sunlight on the drooping rose,
   Or dews within the lily's cup,
Will friendship nurse the hearts of those
   Who hold the treasure up.

A MOTHER'S GIFT.

Verses written in a Bible.

Remember, Son, who gave thee this,
   When other days shall come —
When she, who had thy earliest kiss,
   Sleeps in her narrow home.
Remember 'twas a Mother gave
The gift to one she'd die to save.

A parent's blessing on her son
   Goes with this holy thing.
The love that to the one retain
   Must to the other cling.
Remember, 'tis no idle toy,
A *Mother's gift*, — remember, boy.

A PRAYER.

O, Shepherd of the hosts above,
   Watch o'er thy feeble flock below,
Enfold us in thine arms of love,
   And lead us where Life's waters flow.

O, Lord majestic — 'round whose throne
   The holy chorus ever sing —
Teach us to raise in worthy tone,
   Hosannas to our Saviour-king.

Beneath thine ever watchful eye,
   Within the hollow of thy hand,
O, keep us firm, and when we die
   Receive us in that Better Land.

II. Humorous.

COMFORT.

BY KATE B. T.

A table, with four twisted "limbs," [1]
    Two burners to the gas,
A book complete of Shakespeare's hymns,
    And "something" in a glass;
Peach orchard fire, the blower down,
    Puss purring on the rug,
A rocking-chair, a dressing-gown,
    Nor fitting very snug.

A *bed for one* — a jet of steam
    From hissing kettle's spout,
A key — to shut the one within,
    And shut all others out.
A conscience clear, commandments kept
    Down to the veriest dot,
(Perhaps we'll one or two except,
    We some time have forgot).

---

[1] We should have said "legs," but we bethought ourselves of the Prudes — and so you see we didn't say legs.

No fear of "Master" coming late,
   With most befuddled head,
With maudlin lisp and zigzag gait,
   To roll into our bed;
No rumpus raised, no hue and cry
   From roaring babies — none
That makes the stoutest long to die,
   And go to kingdom come.

No long-tongued females dropping in,
   Heaven keep them from our path;
We'd turn from their unholy grin
   As from the simoon's wrath.
If there's true comfort 'neath the sky,
   When nothing scarce is true,
That home were comfort, so say I,
   Kind reader, what say you?

                    (*N. Y. Despatch.*)

COMFORT.

REPLY TO KATE B. T.

BY WELLY C. W.

A table (with no twisted limbs
   To mar the comely frame);
A book, complete with nursery hymns;
   An *object* for the same;

A tallow dip, by grocers' sold
    As " sixes" to the pound;
A hickory knot to check the cold,
    And send a comfort 'round.

A bed for two, and then, beside,
    A little bed for one —
No room about the house denied
    For little feet to run;
Commandments kept, not only ten,
    But all the others, too,
And " multiply" is one of them —
    Say, Katie, why don't you?

No need of " Paris Lily White,"
    Or " Oriental Flowers,"
To paste the wrinkles out of sight
    For half a dozen hours;
For Nature keeps our cheeks aglow,
    Without the painted dress,
By granting us a constant flow
    Of love and happiness.

No *prude-ent* throes contort our voice,
  Compelling us to say
That limbs are not analogous
  To " legs" in any way;
This only from the lip escapes
  Of maids who always " can,"
But fain would wed a jackanapes,
  " Or any other man."

Jan. 31, 1861.

A LETTER SUPERSCRIPTION.

For *Stamps* I'll bet that Uncle Sam will drop this
    mass of love
At RUFUS WENDELL's domicile, at 37 DOVE,
In ALBANY, N. Y.— and use the best of speed he
    can
To place within the hands of Rufe the " grist" of
    " UNCLE DAN."

TO SISTER LUTHERA.

11 o'clock, evening.

Now here it is so late at night, I *know* it will be hard to write; but then as Addie says I must, I'll do it, and sincerely trust, that I may only keep awake, if merely for the letter's sake.

I hope your *move* is for the best — 'twill surely grant a little rest; one month to visit with your friends, may help a deal to make amends for being housed so long without a chance to move yourself about; and, Thera, when you leave your door remember us at "44;" for, sister, there you'll always find a welcome when you have a mind to call and prove the offer true! What more can anybody do?

Now pray excuse me, for I feel "the drowsy god" doth o'er me steal; and we'll reserve the rest to say when we shall meet some other day.

Your Sleepy Brother,

WELLY.

TO SISTER AURELIA.

ON MOVING TO PHILADELPHIA.

[Albany, May 1, 1870.]

DEAR SISTER REAL:
Your brother's "gone and done it," slick and clean;
He's hired out with Brother Hine to "run" the Howe machine;
But then it's not in Albany (a city, by the way,
That rarely had a *smile* for him), but Phil-a-del-phi-a!

We've let the house in which we live; that's settled, and it's clear
A week or two will find our goods before the auctioneer;
And soon we'll have no house or home, in which we'll care to stay,
Until we settle down for good in Phil-a-del-phi-a.

'Tis probable that I will leave about the first of
    June,
But Addie and the little one will not go down so
    soon;
They'll visit 'round a month or so — go here and
    there a day;
Will *sponge*, and then invite the friends to Phil-
    a-del-phi-a.

Of course, it's hard to leave the friends so long
    " beneath our eye,"
And know the parting's bad enough " to make a
    body cry;"
But then, with steam facilities, it's not so far away,
From native town, or Sturgeondom, to Phil-a-
    del-phi-a.

Now, Sister Real, (and Henry, too,) please bear
    the fact in mind,
You'll find the latch-string hanging out whenever
    you're inclined
To visit brother Welly's folks, for profit or for
    play,
Way down among the Quaker-folks, in Phil-a-
    del-phi-a.

TO CHARLES WENDELL.

[Philadelphia, Sept. 1, 1870.]

Dear Charley, my Cousin, I'm really afraid
Something serious will follow the effort you made
To write Cousin Welly, in measure sublime,
And dress it so neatly in figures and rhyme.

Since reading it, Charley, I'm prone to believe
By a little more practice you would surely achieve
The Laureate's title, his crook and the gown,
And a roosting place clear on the hill of Renown.

Now Charley, stick to it! methinks that afar
I see a faint glimmer — it must be a *Star!*
Yes! and of the first magnitude! Poets, arise!
And hail the new comer — the Queen of the skies!

But, joking aside, Coz, I thank you, and pray
That more such effusions may travel this way;
For it cheers my lone heart! and, perusing, I fain
Would imagine I'm chatting with Charley again.

Your efforts most surely are worthy of praise
In bringing so brightly the *Star* from the haze;
And, if only the clouds of vexation would stay
From its face in the future, there's nought in
 the way.

I am plodding as usual for comfort and bread —
Taking two steps to rear for each one put ahead.
There's a sweet consolation for mortals we
 know —
That is — " over the river " it never is so.

We are well (that's a blessing), but so lonesome
 without
The kind and dear friends we *were* circled about,
That the days come and go like the snail from
 his shell,
And *lonesome, so lonesome's* the story we tell.

You are coming to see us, that's settled it seems,
But WHEN? is the realization of dreams;
Make it *soon* — for it's better the sooner you start,
For we've been *now* too long from each other
 apart.

Our route of procession and order of dress
Will be fully announced through the secular
    press,
Take in the Mint (julep); then, " rounding the
    horn,"
We'll look at the cradle where Freedom was born.

Fairmount and the Park, Girard College, and all
Of the other big sights must come in for a call;
And after we're seen, even down to the least,
We'll partake of a catfish and cantelope feast.

But, resuming the serious — dear Charley, I say,
Couldn't you possibly mention the day
When you and your better half (bless her dear
    heart)
Will be ready to tie up your bundle and start?

Thanks for your letter — please write me another
    one
Fully as long and as sharp as the other one.
Long may your " * " in its glory ascend —
And now a good night to you, Charley, my friend.

KEEP PACE WITH THE TIMES.

Keep pace with the times! let the fogies delay
At the year ago fountain that sets by the way;
Drink you from the water that, crystal and cool,
Progression provides Young America's school.

Keep pace with the times! let the days that are gone
In remembrance be dear — in remembrance alone;
And with cheerfulness clear all the clogs from the way
That would cumber the route of Progression to-day.

Keep pace with the times! get the *best* on the wing —
The *new*, with *improvements*, in everything;
Look about for yourself — nor let fogies instil
Their old-fashioned notions to muddle your will.

Keep pace with the times! the *new Howe* is the queen
Of the family — *the* Sewing Machine;
All others must bow, for the fiat is out —
"The *old* cannot live when the *new* is about."

Keep pace with the times! the NEW HOWE MACHINE
Comes greeting, like sunlight, and throws, by its sheen
Of marvelous beauty and wonderful deeds,
A light from which folly and fogy recedes.

Keep pace with the times! do not tarry or wait
To look at the old things that lie at the gate;
Haste to gaze on the *new*, and we'll warrant you'll say,
"I am glad that I waited to purchase to-day."

I'D RATHER.

I'd rather shake the hardened hand,
    Whose callous comes from honest labor,
Than own the love that seeks to stand
    Above my earnest neighbor.

I'd rather claim companionship
    With honest hearts in rags and stitches,
Than ape the way, or court the lip,
    Of " upper-ten" and riches.

I'd rather deal with one who strives
    Through working days to merit Heaven,
Than trade with those who all their lives
    Crowd labor in the seven.

I'd rather have a country smile —
    Although it comes from hoopless Molly —
Than bear a kiss from " latest style,"
    With furbelows and folly.

April 1, 1867.

BACHELOR'S HALL.

Up two pair of stairs, turn a corner or two,
    Eyes right, lest perchance you encounter a fall,
In tenement four enter softly, and you
    Are within the elysium — Bachelor's Hall.

Examine minutely each object you see,
    From pipes on the stove to the boots on the stand,
And I ween, to a man, that your verdict will be,
    "Not a thing has been touched by a feminine hand."

Here's a cassimer coat sprawling out on the floor,
    With pockets perfumed with tobacco and "sich;"
Where eight buttons should be, you'll discover but four,
    And many a place where is needed a stitch.

Next, over the mirror, all reeking with dirt —
   A stranger for weeks to the wash-woman's tub —
Hangs that glorious symbol — the bachelor's shirt —
   A token of league with the "Bachelor Club."

That vast "curiosity shop" you observe,
   Is the cupboard — a capital vermin retreat;
Index what you find, and its contents will serve
   As a model of every-thing else you may meet.

In short, in the room, from one end to the other,
   Dirt is monarch of all, and disorder is rife;
And we're thankful that fate, with the hand of a mother,
   Has led us away from a Bachelor's life.

ALBANY, Nov. 20, 1859.

A BACHELOR.

You been in love — a bachelor! I'll bet the hock and soda you've merely been a parasite, and shaken for a toady. The passion that you so mistook for love's enchanting power, was self-conceit — the rankest weed that struts the human bower. It's evident, from what you say, that Nature played the wizard, in putting where your heart should be, a lump of fat and gizzard. Begone ye to your den and get your cats and dogs about you; your "fifty loves" have doubtless found they're better off without you. And may Old Time quick take you in, and plant you from the weather; for sure a man with "fifty loves" is ripe enough to gather.

A LESSON

FROM THE GLASS STEAM-ENGINE.

[Prize Poem for which was awarded a Case of Glass Ornaments.]

"Man, know thyself"—all Nature's ways
    Bespeak a lesson, from whose page
Man's mind may learn, throughout his days,
    The beauties of the living age.

So Science, Lit'rature and Art
    In varied chapters strive to show
The onward promptings of the heart,
    That man himself might better know.

Within this gem of crystal light —
    This sport of Fancy's magic hand —
This fount of knowledge and delight
    To old and young throughout the land —

Is blended, in harmonious tone,
    The wondrous with the most sublime,
And much that Art and Science own
    Commingles in this fairy-shrine.

Not like the glass that but reflects
    The shadow and the shape alone,
And curtains all the sad defects
    That long within the heart have grown —

But like the mystic glass portrays
    The *inner* man unmasked, and tells
How man should guard throughout his days
    The temple where the spirit dwells.

O, gem of art, each throbbing beat
    That sends thy crystal arrows out,
Dispels all thought of vain deceit,
    And leaves no witnesses in doubt.

Like thee, may soon our Country stand
    United — one, in peace and power;
Like thee may palsied be the hand
    That dares to smite it from that hour.

    Dec. 27, 1861.

CONQUEST OF THE CONQUEROR.

The shields of Philosophy, Science and Art
Have often been used in defying the dart
From the strong bow of Love; but they never
    would do,
For the metal, though strong, let the arrow go
    through.

Some centuries back (so the story is told)
Aristotle was striving by method to mould
The mind of a pupil — and here let us state,
That pupil became Alexander the Great.

Aristotle could brook no intrusion from Love,
Deeming one so afflicted but little above
The stratum of idiots hard to impress
With truths so essential to honor'd success.

Somehow, with his lessons of wisdom and art,
The subtle admixture of love from the heart
Was blended, which tended, the teacher averred
To keep from the pupil what study conferred.

Alexander — rebuked for his want of a will,
In yielding his heart to the masterly skill
Of Love — sought revenge, and the teacher, they
      say,
Was treated the Homeopathical way.

One day Alexander had managed to place
In position that ranged with the eye and the face,
The lady and great Aristotle the sage,
And left for her eyes the whole battle to wage.

The lady, as worthy a daughter of Eve
As ever has caused a poor Adam to grieve,
Decided to prove the decree but a whim
By making a public example of him.

The battery opens! The tongue and the eyes
Send a legion to take the stronghold by surprise;
And soon, in the wreck of the adamant wall,
Lay Science, Philosophy, teacher and all.

The next cruel step in the conquering plan
Was to make for her service a beast of the man;
And demand, as a proof of his love and esteem,
A ride on his back in the garden at e'en.

Acquiescing, providing some suitable guise
And seclusion should keep from the vulgarly
    eyes
A scene so abasing to prudence and pride,
He'd be the Pegasus for Thalia to ride.

On his hands and his feet, at the beck of an elf,
Aristotle, for Love, made a horse of himself;
Bore the saddle and bit, with the lady as well,
'Till a loud, ringing laugh woke him out from
    the spell.

Alexander, *sub rosa*, had drunk with his eyes
This webbing of Love for a sage and a prize;
Withheld for a season the gushing of mirth,
But the fountain o'erflowed, giving laughter a
    birth.

It has ever been thus, we are prone to believe,
Since Adam partook of the apple with Eve;
Neither Science, Philosophy, Power nor Pride
Can cast all the arrows of Cupid aside.

.

IT'S THE FASHION, DON'T YOU KNOW?

What on earth can be the matter — why this whispering and clatter —
  Like the flow and ebbing patter of the rain upon the roof —
When we ladies at the fading of the sun are promenading,
  Or in quiet esplanading from the masculines aloof?
Can it be the conversation of the male denomination,
  Taking off "abomination" in the way we dress for show?
If in this they find a cancer, we will furnish them a lancer
  In a short but common answer — "It's the fashion, don't you know?"

Though our cheek the hue of roses fresh from where the dew reposes,
  Still they turn their haughty noses — say "it's *nature* not at all;"
And they think they're deuced clever when at punning they endeavor
  Thus to question, "Did you ever see a horse-hair waterfall?"

Up! to arms! the foe's before us — keep the wave from dashing o'er us,
Let's repeat the mighty chorus that shall echo as we go,
" All the mascu-*lie*-ning gender — old or middle, aged or tender —
Must receive the charge we render — "It's the fashion, don't you know?"

Though we rack our brains with scheming — lie awake for fear of dreaming
Something that would be demeaning to our modern views of dress,
Still our modest " quick-accusing " can't prevent the blush suffusing
While they whisper, " You are using none too much — don't make it less."
Well, there's not a use of sighing — let them go on with their dye-ing,
We've a *cause*, there's no denying — and we'll plainly tell them so;
Hark! its echo still is sounding — from the hill tops hear it bounding,
Ev'ry masculine surrounding, " It's the fashion, don't you know?"

THE DOLLAR-MARK.

Money is mighty! Figures look charmlessly
    Unless they are faced with a dollar-mark;
Even the arrows of Justice fall harmlessly
    Before the bold throne of a dollar-mark.
"Twenty thousand" looks large when you write it,
And sounds big to hear one recite it;
But to *know* of its power, unite it
    And call it your own — with a dollar-mark.

Passion can toy with a being at pleasure,
    Backed by the mystical dollar-mark,
Send a death missile, and then, at its leisure,
    Sail on the wings of a dollar-mark.
Then with a patience awaiting
While the law's clamor's abating —
Resting assured that a sating
    Comes with the sign of a dollar-mark.

Pardons and Poverty seldom affiliate,
    Much from the want of a dollar-mark;
Justice and Mercy will rarely conciliate
    Those who are short of the dollar-mark.

If a man errs in society,
Stoops to partake of variety,
Few there are question *his* piety
    While he possesses the dollar-mark.

But there's an ending in ev'ry one's history —
    FINIS, as well, to the dollar-mark;
Yes, and the key to the portals of mystery
    Never's betrayed for a dollar-mark.
Justice, Beyond, is non-buyable;
Judgment, Beyond, is not pliable;
Sentence is sure and reliable,
    Even for lords of the dollar-mark.

May 19, 1871.

MONTOWESE NARROWS;

OR,

THE LEAP FOR LIFE.

With " Dried Huckleberry " Variations.

Ralph! noble heart — with dreams averse
    To sport as found in city's din —
Seeks Branford as vacation's nurse
    For recreations free from sin.

Now Sarah, visiting the place,
    Is sought by one like Ralph of old,
Who reads within her smiling face
    A story that is quickly told.

"To horse! to horse — let's take a 'stray'
    O'er Nature's paths — through blest retreats,"
Says Ralph — while Sarah's willing way
    The invitation quick repeats.

So haps it that, while driving gay
    For Indian Neck in merry ease,
They needs must pass the "narrow way"
    Near by the boarding "Montowese."

Scarce room for one — another team
    Must pass their own — with fear intense
"Whoa! back!" says Ralph — and like a stream
    They rushed the chaise agin the fence.

With view to make discretion's claim
    The better part of valor's worth,
Miss Sarah sought, and not in vain,
    A solid footing on the earth.

Poor Ralph, more scared than hurt, soon brought
    The " rig" to rights upon the road,
When, just as any fellow ought,
    Replaced his pale yet precious load.

North Branford reached — Ralph, leaving S.,
    Strays forth in search of water pure
To quiet Sarah's nervousness,
    And test the praise of water cure.

A house near by, suggests the thought
    The beverage might be tendered him —
A rap — "hallo!" — no answer brought —
    Nor cup to draw the water in.

Undaunted, Ralph searched low and high,
    And not an effort went untried;
Alas! no fruit could he espy,
    Excepting " huckleberries" dried.

So takes he to the waiting S. —
    In place of what he could not raise —
The berries for her nervousness
    While riding in the pleasure chaise.

Who says no virtue can be squeezed
   From " huckleberries" ripe and dried,
Who says a lady can't be pleased
   With " huckleberries" — never tried.

CONEY ISLAND.

(Air.— " *Tramp, Tramp.* ")

When the world is all astir,
   All confusion, all a whirr,
When the tortured brain by not a breeze is fanned,
   What a feeling of relief,
   Though the time be only brief,
'Tis to saunter down to Coney Island strand.

CHORUS.

Come, come, come and let's be marching,
   We'll all be cheery evermore,
And we'll make the welkin ring
While our merry songs we sing
   Of our journey down to Coney Island shore.

We will not forget the day
    When we traveled o'er the way
In the open car — a joyous little band;
    How delightful was the ride
    As we followed with the tide
That was bound for fun and Coney Island strand.

    What a feeling of delight,
    As the ocean came in sight,
And the sun its splendors painted on the sand!
    Oh! 'tis nearly perfect bliss
    To forget the world for this,
And to think alone of Coney Island strand!

    Lay aside the neat attire
    That at home we much admire,
Hook the door that shuts us in and others out,
    Don the bathing dress of blue,
    And, whatever else we do,
Be assured the hooks and buttons are about.

    Now, within the sporting wave,
    How the dancing breakers lave,
As they dash above our heads to reach the shore!
    Oh! we never can forget,
    As the crested lines we met,
How they tumbled all the party o'er and o'er!

Not a king upon his throne —
Not a beggar at his bone —
Not a devotee of Fashion in the land,
Ever knew the half of joy —
Undefiled, without alloy —
Such as bathers find on Coney Island strand.

Thera, self and Kitty D.,
Allen, too, and Linda C.,
We'll remember, as old Time is going o'er,
How the pleasant day was passed
(Hope it will not be the last)
As we journeyed down to Coney Island shore.

FOR THE FUN OF THE THING.

Of course, like the rest of the masculine race,
When a mustache had bloomed on my innocent face,
I presumed I'd a right, with unlimited swing,
To flirt with the girls for the fun of the thing.

Arabella was sweet—such a winsome physique—
Comporting so nicely with every-thing "meek"—
Just humbled my spirit, thus clipping my wing,
And I married the lass for the fun of the thing.

Ah! lackaday! wo, me! each loving caress
Interpreted, cost me a " duck of a dress;"
Phlebotomy tapped at the purse, and the string
Gave way at each call for the fun of the thing.

THE POWER OF EXAMPLE.

AN ARAB TALE.

Nabec, an Arab of that moving race
Who make the desert their abiding place,
Possessed a mare, whose value far outshone,
To him, all wealth of gold or precious stone.

One Daher long had coveted the mare,
Had offered Nabec all his worldly share
Of camels, silks and riches, not the least,
To call his own the " Pride of all the east."

But Nabec loved his desert beauty more
Than Daher's camels, silks, or worldly store;

So turned to all his offers for a trade
A deafened ear. But other plans were laid
By Daher, whereby he could surely gain
The prize, though honest offers were in vain.

"I'll straightway dye my skin another hue,
Gird round my legs a filthy rag or two,
Then by the road, with feign'd distress and grief,
Will wait, like crippled beggar, coming of relief."

Thus wily Daher, garbed in rags and dyed,
Sits by the road, with crutches by his side,
And eagerly awaits, with straining eyes,
The coming Nabec and the coming prize.

Lo! Nabec comes.

"I'm stranger, poor, you see,
Three days have passed and brought no food for
        me,
Unable, being weak with sores and grief,
To look for aid, for comfort or relief."

Good Nabec needs no other rod to touch
His heart, than sickness and a crutch;
So straightway lifts the beggar from the track,
And places him upon the horse's back.

When Daher's hand had grasped the bridle rein,
By speed he hoped to reach the open plain,
While Nabec stood like one within a trance,
Possessed of nothing but his trusty lance,
And heard these words from pseudo-beggar thief:
"Lo! Daher wins! I leave you in your grief;
I've got the mare — I'll ride about at ease,
Go here and there, or anywhere I please."

"Stay!" Nabec cries, "pray list what I've to say:
Thou hast my mare to carry thee away;
Allah so wills, else sure it would not be:
Therefore I wish thee peace, prosperity.
But, I entreat thee, guard thyself with care,
Nor tell to any how thou got'st the mare."

"And, pray," says Daher, "why should I withhold
This method from the ears of young and old?"

" Because, forsooth, some Arab, poor indeed,
Sick, sore and weary, *truthfully* in need,
Might fall beside the way, implore thine arm
To help him home from danger and from harm,
And thou might'st spurn him, harboring the thought,
He puts to practice, what myself hath taught.
Thus would the hand of charity be stayed,
Through fear that want was but a mask that played
Upon the chords within a tender heart,
And help the rogue to get an easy start."

And Daher, struck with Nabec's wise address,
Gave back the mare, and, ready to confess,
Embraced the wronged, and vowed, for time to come,
To prove himself a worthy Arab son.

THE "YANKEE PASS."

One Sabbath morn, some sixty years ago, —
When " going west" was limited, you know,
To Genesee, — two Yankees from a " bout"
Were coming east by Mohawk Valley route.

At early dawn they'd started on their way,
Regardless that 'twas Holy Sabbath day,
When, driving near to Squire Staring's door,
An order came they'd never heard before:
"By virtue of mine office and mine oath,
I now command and order that you both
Get off dose horses, for mine bapers say
I mustn't let you travel on dis day."
"That's plaguy hard," one Yankee quick replied,
"We've been from hum so long; and then, beside,
We've met with none but Indians and the Dutch,
Whose conversation didn't cheer us much.
To be obleeged to stop our travel now,
Is raither worse than all the rest, I swow."
"Yes," says the smaller of the two,
"We mustn't stop, for, surely, if we do
We cannot pay — our purse is very lean —
One dollar and a single pistareen."
Old Squire saw that, if they spoke aright,
It would not pay to keep them over night.
His itching palm and heart so merciless
Much longed the Yankees' dollar to possess;
So, sitting down with them upon the grass,
He promised them an "unmolesting" *Pass*,
Providing they were willing to expend
Their dollar for so privileged an end.

To this they both agreed, and quickly went
With Squire S. to get the document.
Now shrewd old Squire, with sordidness of heart,
Was not expert in calligraphic art,
And Hans, his son, whom honest people claim
Did all the Squire's writing but the name,
Was gone from home; so, turning to the men,
He said: "May be, sirs, you can use the pen,
And write the Pass, for with my name I know
You'll travel free wherever you may go.
I charges but one dollar, which you see
Is what the law allows me as a fee."
The Yankees bowed assent, and with a will
Soon did the task, and, laying by the quill,
Took up the Pass, and in a hurried tone
Read what the Squire thought the quill had done.
The magistrate, (like many now-a-days,)
Gave "honesty" to any man who pays,
Pronounced it right and wrote upon the same
What no one doubted was the Squire's name.
The fee was paid, and, with a quick "good day,"
Our Yankees started on their eastern way;
While Squire chuckled o'er his piece of "tin,"
And how he'd taken two more Yankees in.
A few miles down the Mohawk river's shore
Our Yankees stopped to rest themselves, but more

To turn the "Pass" from paper into gold,
And leave a record of a "Dutchman sold."
Some months elapsed, when Squire happ'ning in
The store of Kanes, the village merchant-man,
Was shown an *order,* and upon the same,
What, unmistaking was the Squire's name;
"Pay 'Zekiel Bartlett and to Samuel Rice
One hundred dollars, and this will suffice
To make you whole, whenever you present
Your claim for cash upon the document."
At first the Squire cast the thing aside
As "goot for nix," "the cussed paper lied,"
And various other Deutscher epithets
Found ventilation, mingled in with threats;
Then came a lull and cogitating vein,
While Squire scanned the pesky thing again,
Gave vent to oath and to the words "Alas!
I knows him now — that tam-ed Yankee Pass."

The sequel proves, as true as Holy Writ,
That oftentimes the "biter" will get bit;
And though a man may claim the Tartar fast,
May find himself the Tartar's man at last.

A FAIR OFFER

FROM JOHN BULL TO MISS COLUMBIA.

Shall we kiss and be friends? Why not sister Columbia,
    No more ugly faces let you and me pull;
Though we both have our tempers, our worries and troubles,
    Let " bygones be bygones " for me says John Bull.

You must own that you've given me a deal of bad language,
    And have been far too free with your bunkum and brag;
That I'll pocket, if now, like a sensible woman,
    You'll disclaim your friend Wilkes, and salute the old flag.

Fools may sneer and call family feelings all humbug,
    But I feel that one blood in the veins of us flows;
Our tongues are the same, though I don't like your fashion
    Of talking (as you'd make *me* pay) through the nose.

We snarled and we scratched in the days of our folly,
    When you wanted to leave me and start for yourself;
To think of those times makes me quite melancholy —
    The blood that we wasted — the temper and pelf!

When I vowed I'd tame you, and make you knock under,
    And you dared me, and bit like a vixen as well;
I did think by this time we had both seen our blunder;
    Meant to live as good friends, and in peace buy and sell.

But of late I can't think what the deuce has come o'er you;
    First you turn your own house out of the window and then
Declare that I want to o'er-reach you and floor you —
    Stop my ship, seize my passengers, bully my men!

I can stand a great deal from my own blood relations,
    And I know that your troubles your temper have soured;
But I can't take a blow, in the face of all nations,
    And consent to see law by brute force overpowered.

Only own your friend Wilkes is a blundering bully,
    And make over Mason and Slidell to me,
And all that is past I'll condone fair and fully,
    Kiss you now, and in future, I do hope agree.

— London Punch.

REPLY

OF MISS COLUMBIA TO JOHN BULL.

I'll accept, brother John, of your proffered re-union,
   By tendering kisses for every blow,
With the prayers of my children, in thankfulness given,
   That the "squabble" has caused not a blood-drop to flow.

But I vow, brother John, you've a deal of the "brazen,"
   In playing the *plaintiff* with blustering grace,
And declaring with splenitive flashes, that sooner
   Than grant me a favor, you'll spit in my face.

O, yes, brother John, I remember the snarling
   And scratching and biting by you rudely done,
When yet but an infant I battled your legions,
   And swore, though an infant, to " go it alone."

I know, brother John, what has caused the re-
   action,
   And stirred up the bile that so sourly fills
You to day — not the want of a feeling,
   But the want of my cotton for running your
      mills.

Now, my dear brother John, it illy becomes you
   To don with bravado the mien of a saint,
And prate with such gusto, my battle for Union
   Is coupled with horrors, no mortal can paint.

O, for shame, brother John, let your little
      "Lord" Russell
   Hide his head, which is nearly of reason bereft,
While we read the black page of your India tussel,
   In the letters he penned and the record he left.

Though we seek, brother John, to preserve a
      relation
   Of amity with you for ages to come,
You can not, by Bull-ying, break up our nation,
   Or cause a relax till our labor is done.

ACROSTIC.

Sweet to love when every token,
Tried by friendship still unbroken,
Over ills the most provoking, conquering with a
magic power,
Round thy name a memory clingeth,
Radiating light it bringeth,
Sorrow fades when friendship singeth, "Love me
from this hour."

OLD PAT IS DEAD!

Poor Dog "Pat."— General grief is expressed over the death of this poor canine, whose familiar face, for upwards of twelve years, has greeted the guests at the Stanwix and Merchants' Hotels. "Pat" was known to many of the traveling public, by whom his demise, at the age of 17, will be as deeply felt, as by the author of the following lines, dedicated to the memory of "Pat," who has gone to join "Poor Dog Tray:"

Old Pat is dead! Old age apace
Crept on, and gave to death's embrace
Another dog who'd had his day,
And then from trouble passed away.

For friends Old Pat had never lacked,
In rat-crusades was freely backed;
'Tis true at some he'd bark, but then
Was always kind to gentlemen.

In peace Old Pat is now at rest,
No more to greet the coming guest,
And if Dog-Heaven can be found,
You'll find Old Pat there, running 'round.

ALBANY, Oct. 11, 1869.

III. Patriotic.

THE SOLDIER'S GOOD BYE.

Good bye to you, mother!
   Though hard is the parting —
Though sad is the picture
   That gleams in your eye —
Let your love for your boy
   Check the tear at its starting —
Here's my hand with my heart
   To be faithful. Good bye!

Good bye to you, father!
   Remember and cherish
My vow — that has cost,
   Perhaps, many a sigh —
To be zealous and loyal —
   And then, should I perish,
You'll remember I died
   For my country. Good bye!

Good bye to you, sister!
  The sun on the morrow
May be laden with gladness
  In every ray,
Yet no joy will suffice
  In dispelling the sorrow
Of thus parting with you,
  My dear sister to-day.

Good bye to you, brother!
  The deepest dejection
Comes crowding upon me
  In taking your hand;
But a solace I find
  In the single reflection,
That I leave you for service
  In Liberty's band.

Good bye to you, darling!
  The vows that we've spoken,
Will be sealed with my love for you
  Down in my breast;
I hope to return
  With their pledges unbroken,
And find with you home
  For a soldier to rest.

Good bye to you, friends!
   Should my ardent devotion
Decree for me death
   And a patriot's grave,
You'll remember I lived
   For my country's promotion,
And died for the liberty
   WASHINGTON gave.

ALBANY, Oct. 18, 1861.

THE DYING VOLUNTEER.[1]

Kneel closer, brother, for I feel my life is ebbing fast;
Kneel closer, for to-day, you know, will surely be my last;
I cannot part, I cannot die unless I hear you tell
That I have loved my country and have served my country well.

---

[1] Was set to music by Boyd, and published by Ditson & Co., Boston, and had an extensive sale.

O, could I hear my father's voice just speaking
    to me now;
O, could I feel my mother's hand just laid upon
    my brow;
O, could my sister's love but move this moisture
    from my eye,
I'd ask no other boon than this — then, like a
    soldier, die.

When death shall still this throbbing heart and
    close these feeble eyes,
Just promise, brother, ere my soul departs for
    yonder skies,
To tell my mother how the love she kindled in
    my breast,
When in the tent or battle-field, surmounted all
    the rest.

Yes, tell her that her parting words I never could
    forget;
I hear them ringing in my ears — I feel them
    burning yet;
And with the pledge I made her then stepped
    boldly in the strife,
To God I gave my heart, and for my country gave
    my life.

I'm going home — not where the gems in circles
    set with love,
Are sparkling 'round the parent crown — but
    going home above;
Where jewels shine with richer light, not bor-
    rowed from the sun:
Where blood and war can never reach — the home
    of WASHINGTON.

ALBANY, Feb. 27, 1862.

LETTER

To CAPT. NELSON O. WENDELL.[1]

(Then a Non-Commissioned Officer in the 44 N. Y. Vols.)

ALBANY, N. Y., Dec. 15th, 1861.

DEAR UNCLE NELSON:

I received in due season, your last, and the reason I've neglected to answer it is, by the way, that chronic disease of taking my ease and delaying 'till morrow the work of to-day.

---

[1] Capt. Nelson O. Wendell, commanding Co. F., 121st N. Y. Vols., was killed in battle at Salem Heights, Va., on the 3d of May, 1863. [See Appendix.]

But from you, Uncle Nelse, more than any-
one else, I love to receive an occasional letter;
and I'm sure, could you fight as well as you write,
our country would speedily change for the better.

In the army for right that is waiting to-night
with an ardent desire to grapple the foe; I am
sure, not a man in our "Liberty's clan" is im-
bued with a loftier spirit than you.

I am happy to know it *agreed* with you so to
receive the small favor we sent you by mail, and
we only regret we have not as yet, sent you something more *comforting* " over the rail."

Our boys at Fort Pickens, have been raising
the "Dickens" with the chivalric (?) sons under
traitorous Bragg, and the future will tell how
they "peppered them well," while above them
still floated America's flag.

I showed Charley the letter you wrote, and a
better and more punctual nephew he has promised
to be; I suppose you'll believe, if you ever receive a letter to prove what he's promised to me.

Bert has written again and he says the *camp-
pain*, which had *spirit* enough but lacked comfort
and ease; has most welcomely beat a *rheumatic* retreat and left him a master of elbow and knees.

May you ever *Revere*,[1] and, regardless of fear, bear in triumph our banner all over the land; and, with *Stryker*,[2] we know you will foster the blow that will *strike her* traducers on every hand.

Both my wife and the other (which used to be such a bother to you when you sought for a little respite) say "please tell Uncle Nell we are wishing him well, and wish he was here with us sitting to-night.

May the Heavenly arm keep you safely from harm; guide our army by land and our navy by sea; cause rebellion to quake, and finally make *one* circle of States as the home of the FREE.

Respectfully yours,
W. C. W.

FREEDOM'S GIFT.

When the Oak of the Union — whose majesty
    towers
  Above the dynasties and thrones of the world —
First bent to the blast of Secession, and showers
  Of wrath by the minions of Slavery hurled;

---

[1] Capt. Revere. [2] Col. Stryker.

The Union's defenders in legions assembled
   And planted themselves at the foot of the tree,
Proclaimed in a voice, at which Tyranny trembled,
   "All these, Oh! my Country, we tender to thee."

From the hives on the shores of the mighty Atlantic —
   From the blossoming fields of the Orient's pride —
To the banks where the new El Dorado romantic
   Hurls back the wild waves that are lashing her side —
Came the tread of a host, through the Nation resounding
   And they marched 'neath the folds of the flag of the free;
Came a shout, and whose echo e'en now is rebounding,
   "These breasts, Oh! my Country, we offer to thee."

The purse of the "million," unloosed by the thunder
  That shook the foundations of towers of gold,
Accepting the issue that rent it asunder,
  In the lap of the Nation its power unrolled.
The heart of the People, in anticipation
  Of a dawning to-morrow from Tyranny free,
Beat time, while recording its firm declaration,
  "All this, Oh! my Country, we offer to thee."

There is many a light from the cot and the palace
  Gone out, but to dazzle in glory above;
And many an offering dropped in the chalice
  With tears from the Heavenly fountain of Love.
Yet the bow in its splendor is rising before us,
  While Hope buoys the hearts on the land and the sea,
And the *Nation* in harmony joins in the chorus,
  "All these, Oh! my Country, we offer to thee."

WHAT THE BOYS IN BLUE SAY.

For the Albany Evening Journal.

Hear what the boys in blue say: "Yes, Treason is a crime
That should be rendered odious in ev'ry age and clime;
And even death can scarce efface the sin — so dark its hue."
That's what the boys in blue say — the noble boys in blue!

Hear what the boys in blue say: "We've passed the stern ordeal,
Through seas of blood to help maintain our blessed country's weal,
We want no traitor's hand to guide — we've plenty that are true."
That's what the boys in blue say — the honest boys in blue.

Hear what the boys in blue say : " What ! truckle at the shrine
Whose corner stone rests on the bones of friends of yours and mine ?
Back ! Treason ! thou art odious ! in vain to plead or sue."
That's what the boys in blue say — the trusty boys in blue.

Hear what the boys in blue say : " These mateless limbs remind
How treason plucked the life from out the ones we left behind ;
But, single-handed, crutched and lame, we'll fight the battle through."
That's what the boys in blue say — the loyal boys in blue.

Hear what the boys in blue say : " No tongue that murmured 'Pause,'
When we were hurling back the hosts of that unholy cause,
Shall speak for us in Congress halls, nor tell us what to do."
That's what the boys in blue say — the sturdy boys in blue.

Hear what the boys in blue say: "We own no kith or kin
    With those who claim that Treason is a pardonable sin;
No! sweep the monster from the land — whatever else you do!"
That's what the boys in blue say — the earnest boys in blue.

Now what the boys in blue say will swell the mighty strain,
Whose primal notes have just been heard from loyal-loving Maine;
And when November calls New York to do her duty too,
In thunder tones the boys will speak — the noble boys in blue.

ALBANY, Sept. 24, 1866.

TO NORTHERN PEACEMAKERS.

Back! deriders of the Nation,
Laughers at the desolation
Treason brought upon the people, once united,
    happy, free;
Retribution for the sorrow,
In hereafter's glad to-morrow,
Must be shared alike by traitors and abettors such
    as ye.

Back! and hear ye not the thunder
Talking "Peace" from over yonder,
Just adown the fertile valley Early[1] dared to
    desolate;
"Peace" from every sabre gleaming;
"Peace" from every banner streaming;
Guaranteeing Peace forever to the people and the
    State.

"Back!" comes surging o'er the mountain —
Sherman sends it from the fountain

---

[1] Confederate Gen. Early.

Whereat Treason oft replenish'd gaping mouths
    with shot and shell,
  Nothing less than full submission,
  And our Union's recognition,
Are the terms of peace he offers where our
    brothers fought and fell.

  Back! Oppression's petted creature;
  Hideous in every feature;
Born to truckle to the tyrant, and to bow obse-
    quiously,
  Echoes from the thousands sleeping,
  Glistens in the tears we're weeping,
Speaks from many vacant places in this home of
    Liberty.

  Back! the Olive branch ye tender
  Clothed with peacefulness and splendor
Bears the buds foretelling fruit of bitter Discord's
    fated tree!
  We will offer them the flower
  In its majesty and power
When they gather with their sisters around the
    tree of Liberty!

Victory is just before us;
Hear ye not the noble chorus
Wafted from Old Salamander's iron troop of shot
    and shell,
And where Jeff himself is planted,
Every wish will soon be Grant-ed,
When beneath the starry banner Treason hears
    its funeral knell.

Indiana, Maine, Ohio
Firm for truth — a noble trio —
Standing by the Union banner, swear eternal
    fealty;
Pennsylvania, in thunder,
Warns the foe to stand from under.
Back! ye traitors who would trample on the en-
    sign of the free!

WELCOME PEACE.

Come, welcome Peace — exert thy reign —
  So let thy glorious power shine,
That trodden fields shall bloom again,
  And blushing fruit depend the vine.

Come, nurture in the Nation's heart
   A brother's love, and let it be
The chord whose music forms a part
   Of Freedom's blessed symphony.

Come, let our noble banner wave —
   Its colors adoration meet —
And only him be held a slave
   Who tramples it beneath his feet.

Come, welcome Peace, so nerve the hand —
   So tune the heart and fill the breast
Of him who soon shall rule the land,
That all may rise and call him blest.

THE RETURN OF PEACE.

The cloud has passed — the gladd'ning rays
   Already edge with welcome light
' The morning of the peaceful days;
   Yes, 'tis no longer night.

The measured tread of friend and foe
   Is hushed in desolation's track,
The tide of blood has ceased to flow
   And States are coming back.

ALBANY Jan. 1, 1866.

KANSAS AND FREEDOM.

Freeman of the North, awake — Kansas loudly calls for thee
To protect her virgin soil from the curse of Slavery;
Vindicate your love of freedom, love of justice and of right,
By declaring Kansas never shall be blackened with the blight.

Trusty men with trusty rifles hasten to the field of strife,
Love of freedom be your armor — have no fears of losing life,
Face the king of chains and bondage — drive the lion to his lair,
Vow that liberty and justice shall be reared and nurtured there.

Though we sought for intercession at the seat of ruling
    power,
When the hostile clouds were thick'ning and o'er Kansas
    seemed to lower,
Deaf to every supplication — blind to wrong's aggressive
    sway —
Mute to every cry of freedom — Franklin[1] turned our plea
    away.

Men baptized at Freedom's altar — sturdy yeoman bold
    and free —
Vowed to consecrate the irbeing at the shrine of Liberty;
Wrong, though clad in gilded armor, sanctioned by the rul-
    ing rod,
Right will bow the mighty giant, tho' it wade through seas
    of blood.

Hasten, friends of truth and justice — Kansas needs a help-
    ing hand,
Fearless hearts to face the tyrant — willing men to till the
    land.
Guard with love the family altars dedicated to the free,
Let the plains of Kansas echo loudly shouts of " Victory."

---

[1] An Allusion to President Pierce.

TO THE XLth CONGRESS.

X L, in framing laws to guide
    Our nation through the troubled sea,
X L, in Peace — the nation's pride —
    X L, in love and unity.

X L, in branding Treason, *crime* —
    Though sugar coat it as they may,
With hope to spare in future time
    His X, L, N, C, & D, J.

IV. Political

MATCH HIM.[1]

Grant the hero's on the course;
    Match him, match him.
Democrats from any source,
    Match him if you can.
You are sure to meet the wall,
In the vote the coming Fall —
Grant is bound to beat you all,
    Match him if you can.

Chorus.

Then rally, boys, for the good old Union,
    Union! Union!!
Then rally, boys, for the good old Union,
    Hip, hip, hurrah!

---

[1] A Campaign Song, set to music by Andrew Boyd, published by Ditson & Co., Boston, and extensively sung by various Glee Clubs.

"See, the conquering hero comes,"
    Match him, match him ;
Sound your trumpets, beat your drums,
    Match him if you can.
Unpretending, full revealed,
Firm as on the battle field —
"Forward, boys, we'll never yield,"
    Match him if you can.

      CHORUS.— Then rally, boys, etc.

"Peace" surrounds our candidate,
    Match him, match him,
"Hope" is knocking at the gate,
    Match him if you can.
Choose from Democratic "stars,"
Heroes of the triple bars —
We present the "Son of Mars,"
    Match him if you can.

      CHORUS.— Then rally, boys, etc.

"Boys in Blue" the challenge fling,
    Match him, match him ;
Echo makes the welkin ring,
    "Match him if you can."

Crippled by the rebel's hate,
Taunted in a Northern State,
They present a candidate,
   Match him if you can.

     CHORUS.— Then rally, boys, etc.

Grant's the man to "fight it out,"
   Match him, match him;
He will put the foe to rout,
   Match him if you can.
Grant is on a mission bent,
To the White House from the tent —
Grant shall be our President,
   Then match him if you can.

     CHORUS.— Then rally, boys, etc.

ALBANY, July, 1868.

MARCHING ALONG.

Respectfully dedicated to the "Unconditionals" of Albany.

The loyal are gath'ring from near and from far,
In Peace they're a host, as they were in the War;
With GRANT their commander, the Union their song,
There's naught can prevent them from marching along.

CHORUS.
Marching along, we are marching along,
With GRANT for our leader we are marching along;
Our watchword is ringing, 'tis "Down with the wrong,
And up with the banner," we are marching along.

The foe that's before us we know is the same
We met on the mountains, in valley and plain;
Our banner in triumph prevailed o'er the wrong,
And now with the ballot we're marching along.

The Union defenders are speaking again —
In echoes of thunder we hear them in Maine;
Vermont boys have proven to whom they belong,
With GRANT on their banners they're marching along.

Then hail to the chieftain, hurra for the man
Whose work disconcerts all that Rebels may plan;
A name that is worthy of labor and song —
For GRANT and the Union we're marching along.

ALBANY, Sept., 1868.

WHEN GRANT GOES MARCHING IN.

AIR — "*When Johnny comes marching home.*"

Vermont has spoken out again,
  Hurra, Hurra!
We've heard the glorious news from Maine,
  Hurra, Hurra!
In thunder tones the people spake,
And made the walls of Treason shake,
  They'll all come down
    When Grant goes marching in.

With Grant to lead the loyal band,
  Hurra, Hurra!
We'll drive Rebellion from the land,
  Hurra, Hurra!

Horatio and the Forrest crew
Will surely find enough to do,
   They'll all come down
     When Grant goes marching in.

The starry flag shall monarch be,
   Hurra, Hurra!
O'er all the States from sea to sea,
   Hurra, Hurra!
The Seymourites may raise their flag,
With bars of Treason on the rag,
   They'll all come down
     When Grant goes marching in.

The good old Ship will safely ride,
   Hurra, Hurra!
With Grant to pilot — Grant to guide,
   Hurra, Hurra!
No traitor light is heeded now,
No hidden rock to strike the prow,
   They're all wiped out
     Since Grant went marching in.

Now boys we'll work though shine or rain,
   Hurra, Hurra!
Until November comes again,
   Hurra, Hurra!

We'll show the rebels that the man
Who leads Secession's wicked clan,
   Must stand one side,
  For Grant is marching in.

GLORY HALLELUJAH.

We're on the road to victory and laurels will increase,
For Uncle Sam has given us the Yankee Doodle lease,
With GRANT — the "Unconditional" — to lead the way
    to peace,
  We're sure in marching on.
 Glory, glory, hallelujah; Glory, glory, hallelujah,
 Glory, glory, hallelujah, we're sure in marching on.

Jeff Davis didn't hang upon the "sour apple tree,"
But loyalty has branded him with lasting infamy!
In plucking out the traitor weeds that cumber liberty,
  We still are marching on.

GRANT put the rebel fire out, though fed with Northern hate;
He whipped the Rebs in '62, and will in '68.
To make him our President and take the chair of State,
  We now are marching on.

Then join the loyal army in its mission for the right;
Prosperity and Plenty are the trophies of the fight;
The sun of Peace will gladden soon the nation with its
    light,
  As we go marching on.

ALBANY, 1868.

GRANT AND THE UNION.

Respectfully dedicated to the "Unconditionals," of Albany.

AIR — "*Down in a Coal Mine.*"

I am a loyal Union man,
  And surely love to see
Each honest heart do what he can,
  Wherever he may be,
To fling our banner to the breeze
  And give it constant care,
Until our Nation and its flag
  Is honorèd ev'ry-where.

Chorus.

Grant and the Union! let the echo sound!
Union forever, boys, pass the toast around;
Treason must surrender, for *we* never shall,
And our terms are "Unconditional."

We have a Captain at the head
   We know will never yield
To Treason at the Capital,
   Or rebels in the field.
We know for him secession bent
   On mountain, hill and plain;
We've tried him once for President,
   We'll try him once again.

The tremble of the Greeley-ites,
   Is just before the fall,
Each rally-effort only lights
   The "writing on the wall;"
And when November comes again,
   As ev'ry thing denotes,
They'll find their *weigh* and cause to be
   A little short of votes.

ALBANY, Sept. 3, 1872.

MARCHING ALONG.

The harvest is ready, and rich is the yield
We'll gather for truth from the National field;
We'll tramp down the stubble, the tares and the wrong,
And garner the loyal while we're marching along.

Chorus.

Marching along, we are marching along;
With GRANT for our leader, we are marching along —
Our watchword is ringing — it is "Down with the wrong,
And up with the banner," we are marching along.

For GRANT and for WILSON, for DIX and TREMAIN,
We'll shout from the mountains, the valley and plain;
And to all there is welcome to join in the song —
So gird on your armor and be marching along.

Then hail to the chieftain, hurrah for the man
Whom no one has beaten, and nobody can;
Whose sword is a terror to Treason and Wrong —
For GRANT and the Union we are marching along.

Sept., 1872.

V. Carriers' Addresess.

WE GREET YOU.

[Jan. 1, 1868.]

We've turned another yearly leaf within the
    Book of Time —
The record of our joys and woes — of happiness
    and crime.
To some with peace the year has died — to some
    perhaps with tears,
But '67 rests within the Sepulchre of Years.

" A Happy New Year" — merry chimes — from
    old and young its ring
Glides in to make melodious the merry songs they
    sing.
" A Happy New Year unto all — in rags or match-
    less fur ! "
This greeting take in welcome from the Letter
    Carrier.

The Carrier breasts the beating storm, the cold,
    the burning ray;
With duty seeks to blend the joy of pleasing day
    by day,
The welcome bridge of Uncle Sam, o'er which
    your letters glide
From Post o'er countless steps to reach your
    happy fireside.

"A Happy New Year!" Gently, Time, deal with
    the good and fair;
Keep back the furrows from the face and silver
    from the hair!
Let joy and peace our Country fill, through City,
    Town and State:
Adieu to '67 and Hurrah for '68!

Second Part.

Kind friends! while Time is forward fleeting,
The LETTER CARRIER sends you greeting,
And wishes, as his song he sings you,
A blessing on the news he brings you.

Your CARRIER well might boast of knowledge,
(He goes so oft through School and College;)
But learning's rules he counts as fetters,
And only seeks to " know his LETTERS ! "

Tho' " notes" and " numbers" he must balance,
Your CARRIER claims no poet's talents,
And therefore hopes he may not bore you,
When with his " lines" he *halts* before you.

The man who " drops a word in season,"
Is said to show both wit and reason ;
If so, the CARRIER does much better,
Who " drops in season" every " LETTER."

Remember friends, with due reflection,
The CARRIER goes by your " DIRECTION ; "
Your " NAME" for him has such attraction,
He lives by " corresponding" action.

He follows you — he seeks you often,
Your hopes to raise, your cares to soften ;
By winter chilled, by summer roasted,
He reads and runs to keep you " POSTED."

So, while the New Year Season blesses,
The Carrier drops his brief " addresses ; "
And though he writes no learned thesis,
He hopes that his " Delivery" pleases.

May all your friends, with tender feeling,
Be like good Envelopes, " Self Sealing ; "
And all your business, closely heeded,
Provide you " Stamps" whenever needed.

" These Lines," with New Year's salutations,
Come from your friends of various " Stations,"
And that our toils may all be Re-paid,
" Please answer by return post" Pre-paid.

The Letter Carriers.

CARRIERS' ANNUAL GREETING.

Albany Evening Journal.

[Jan. 1, 1869.]

"Happy New Year, Happy New Year" —
Send the echo down the line;
Bells are ringing, voices singing
Praises to the year beginning;
Join we in the cheering chorus,
Welcoming the year before us;
"Happy New Year, Happy New Year,
Welcome Eighteen Sixty-Nine."

Though wind may howl, and sleet or driving rain,
Or hail beat tattoos on the window pane;
Though frost may wed itself to snowy flake,
And audibly, with ev'ry step we take
Speak words whose coldness leaves the biting sting
And telegraphs to teeth a chattering :
Still, though we know the wintry wind blows chill,
Yet storm or cold brings not the Carrier ill,

If your warm hearts but feel a quicker flow
Of ruddy life and news-awakened glow
At our approach. Our mission is to please
The laborer, and gentleman of ease —
The one whose muscle, brain and sweating brow
Turns sod for Progress with an earnest plow,
And him whose purse — the garner of the seed —
Unloosens as the fields of Progress need.

 In one short year what changes have been wrought,
Some days with pleasure, some with sorrow fraught;
Some hearts with joy have leaped at Fortune's smile,
Some, sorrow-stricken, pined away the while.
 "Sweet Sixteen" laughs and prates in highest glee —
Time gives her charms he takes from "Twenty-three;"
While fading beauty lingers at the glass,
And sighs and moans "I am no more *a-lass.*"
The youthful master doffs the cap and kirtle,
And deems himself a rose and not a myrtle;
Strokes up the down that struggles on his chin
And swears the barber must his task begin.

With "frenzy uncontrollable" he seeks
To bury deep with hair the ruddy cheeks;
And should, perchance, but Nature dare deny
The color *black*, he straightway seeks to *dye*.
Balls, parties, concerts, perfumes and cigars
Crowd his weak noddle with a thousand cares;
With faultless tie and kids immaculate —
The Grecian Bend an aptly chosen mate —
Make room, ye masses! see ye not the Page
That Folly sends with Fashion's equipage?
The prime old bach, bankrupt in hope and heart,
Sees happiness, but with it has no part;
While wedded love, perhaps, has found too soon
The transient mock'ry of the honeymoon.
Sly, artful Cupid's had abundant sport
Preparing cases for the special court;
Has found as many soft and yielding hearts
As ever felt the power of his darts.

   But, pardon me, kind reader, for not here
Can I review those changes of the year
Which came and went, as slyly as the dew,
And found no record in my day's review.
My task it was Life's varied scenes to scan
And learn new lessons from the deeds of man;
Or with the Poets to beguile the hour,
And cull the ones most fragrant in the bower.

I've daily told you by the printed page
How swept the floods and where the fires rage;
Where roaring hail storms threshed the harvest
    field,
And when King Frost the Autumn fountain
    sealed.
How rosy Spring danced o'er the meadows green,
And crystal brooks ran flow'ry banks between:
With poet-wreath I bound her pleasant brow
And hung rhymed garlands on a rustic plow;
Till when on high the dog-star, hot and red,
His scorching influence over Summer shed.
In their unceasing circle tripped the seasons
Bringing strange incidents, suggesting reasons,
Which all within my open columns found
A lodgment for my waiting readers 'round.
I've told you how, upon a distant shore,
A city was, a city is no more;
How quaking earth and monster tidal wave
Brought multitudes to an unthinking grave.
I've told of murders, riots and of wars,
Discordant States, and wild Ambition's jars;
And then again of matters nearer home
I've talked the year around, and what was done.
Not only have the rough and broken acts
Of stubborn life been mine, and stubborn facts,

But here and there a wreath by fancy twined,
Like gloomy clouds, with gold and silver lined,
Drawn out in 'witching story, 'guiling thought,
With Cupid's pranks and freaks well inter-
    wrought;
Of terror-mantled tale of breathless dread,
O'er fascinating pages strangely spread;
All acts of all mankind, all fortunes, fates,
All accidents and incidents and dates.

    Now that we've passed the mystic line
        And closed the yearly gate,
    We'll not forget in Sixty-Nine
        To think of Sixty-Eight.
    A thousand little thoughts of some
        Can find an active play
    By turning leaves and dating from
        A year ago to-day.

    The records of a single year
        Are strangely interwrought
    With life and death, with hope and fear,
        With gay and gloomy thought.

But few can turn the pages o'er
    With truthfulness and say
"I've many friends, and had no more
    A year ago to-day."

Not many eyes that now behold
    The dawning of the year
Have not been witnesses that told
    The story of a tear;
Not many hearts but what can claim
    Companionship with clay
That held a soul within its frame
    A year ago to-day.

How many who essayed to climb
    Ambition's giddy mount,
Have fallen in this little time,
    None will attempt to count,
Yet Power, Gold and Lucifer,
    Can shout aloud and say,
"As many follow as there were
    A year ago to-day."

AMERICA! the Mecca of the world —
Toward whose shores so many ships unfurled
Their sails in years before, and millions bless'd
With peace in homes of Liberty and rest —
Still opens wide its arms, and all who will
May come within and find a welcome still.
Broad acres yet are waiting for the plow,
And forests want the axe to make them bow.
The West still calls, from mountain, plain and glen,
For millions more of Nature's Noblemen.

Though for a time the cloud of war and hate
In darkness left our noble ship of state,
The sun of Peace the brighter seems to smile
For being veiled with gloominess awhile.
It set, and with it heroes found a grave;
It rose, and with it rose no shackled slave.

Unknown to fame, but with a dauntless zeal,
Behold a hero leads the Great Appeal —
Makes Treason blush with shame and quickly find
The potent power of a Master Mind.
Our noble GRANT — unschooled to know defeat —
Stands by the flag and makes the work complete;

Speaks words in deeds and acts of common sense
That charms the world with mighty eloquence.
To him, whose name will reach beyond to-day,
And proudly live when years have rolled away,
We point with pride; and, fresh from out the tent,
The People's voice has made him President.
With Peace to light the future, who shall say
" A greater is" than our America.

A thought for the dead and a sigh with the weep-
 ing,
 'Tis fitting we give at the birth of the years,
To the heroes that fell and as heroes are sleeping
 In graves never wet with affectionate tears.

" I miss," says the mother, " my boy at the table,
 I miss him as year after year passes by;
But O, I shall see him, and while I am able,
 I'll cling to the rock that is higher than I."

" E'en though not a stone nor a flower or willow
 Can point me the place where the mortal may
 lie,
I am sure that good angels are watching his pil-
 low —
 I'll cling to the rock that is higher than I."

"Deep, deep in my heart, with the purest devotion,
  Embalmed for my life as a hero you lie —
With a faith that can conquer the wildest commotion,
  I'll cling to the rock that is higher than I."

O, ye who are blessed from the rich flowing fountain
  Of Plenty and Happiness, add to your cheer,
By helping to move the disconsolate mountain
  That keeps from the stricken a Happy New Year.

Lo! sluggish Spain, long gyved, essayed to be
Unshackled from the toils of Tyranny;
With little strife won to herself the day,
Despoiled the Throne and sent the queen away;
While Freedom dawned, and with effulgent light
Broke in upon the centuries of night.
  Untutored in the school of Liberty,
Perchance this quick and signal victory
May yet delay the boon of life to Spain,
And send her back to monarchy again.
May He who holds the Nations in His hand
Proclaim that Liberty shall rule the land.

Spasmodic France successive haps betide
To check Ambition's mad and reckless stride,
And will so long as minion holds the voice
And makes a slave of ev'ry good bourgeois.
Napoleon reads in ev'ry word and tread
Monitions of a shower overhead.
A muzzled Press its potent power wields
E'en in its silence, and the monarch feels
Unstable on his throne. The leaven set
By hero BAUDIN works and rises yet.

Sink as you will the germ of Human Right —
Deny the sun of Liberty its light —
Forbid the rain of love to feel its way
Down through the clods of years' despotic clay;
Yet there's a Power thrones cannot suppress,
Nor tomes of edicts make a whit the less;
A Power meet to break the bonds of night,
And give the germ its liberty and light.

From north to south, from west unto the east,
The People's Voices start monarchs from the feast,
And on the wall of Destiny appears
In words indellible, "The Tyrant's years
Are numbered," and the dawning ray
Proclaims the coming of the Better Day.

The Yankee Nation — what a race!
On earth there's no abiding place,
No mountain, valley, plain or wood
But where a Yankee foot has stood.
The Pyramids have e'en essayed
To trust a Yankee in its shade;
He's felt the wild and cooling breeze
That plays about the Pyrenees;
E'en where the Alps in grandeur rise
With snowy caps to pierce the skies,
His restless tread has left the trace
Of foot-prints from the Yankee race.
Now in the fields of ice and snow —
The home of seals and Esquimaux —
He seeks to know how large a hole
Surrounds the mystic Northern Pole,
And strives to prove it if there be
In truth an open Polar sea.
You'll find him in the Eastern khan,
That shelters either beast or man;
Or down among the silks and teas
Of Chinamen and Japanese.
Now, with this penchant " more to know,"
If *this* or *that* be *thus* and *so*,
Forsooth who knows but he may soon
Be climbing mountains in the moon.

And now, my kind patrons, my rhyming must
    cease:
May each day's succession but only increase
Your measure of happiness, plenty and cheer —
I bid each and all of you " Happy New Year."

SECOND ANNUAL ADDRESS.

[January 1, 1870.]

With the years of the Past we have added another,
    Sixty-nine is at rest, and it surely is clear
That to each man and woman, friend, sister or
    brother,
    Old Time, as a Carrier, leaves a New Year.

With edging of bright days the cloudlets of sorrow
    Lose half of the terror a fullness would show;
So the Carrier wishes to-day and to-morrow
    Your clouds may be few, with the edges aglow.

The wonders of wire-talk still are increasing;
    Like tendrils the Telegraph seeks to embrace
The whole of the earth, with a vigor unceasing,
    Till the Orient speaks with the Occident race.

But your " self-sealing" missives of love and affec-
    tion,
  When brought you by mail, win your confi-
      dence more,
And you're certain to cherish, with fond recollec-
    tion,
  The time that the Carrier's due at your door.

" Here's a letter for you, sir, mailed from a station
    Not afar from your own, sir — it's brimming
      with cheer;
It is not a tirade from a friend or relation,
    But it's right to the point, sir — ' a Happy New
      Year.'"

"Here's another for madame, ' my lady,' or
      misses —
  Not *private*, but open, explicit and clear;
You may not find in it *my dear*-ings or kisses,
  But the Carrier's wishes, 'a Happy New Year.'"

With a duty to do, and a will to assist him,
    The Carrier tramps to that music alone;
No storm can prevent and no pleasure enlist him,
    To swerve from the path 'till that duty is done.

Here's health to the new-born, success to its
 reigning;
Full be its record of plenty and cheer;
And here's that the " Finis" may find you remain-
 ing,
And here's to each one of you " HAPPY NEW
 YEAR."

Appendix.

CAPT. NELSON O. WENDELL.

In Memoriam.

[The following papers are placed in the present volume as a merited tribute to a memory that will long be affectionately cherished by a wide circle of relatives and friends. The first is an Obituary sketch which appeared, in May, 1863, in the editorial columns of the *Mohawk Valley Register*, of Fort Plain, N. Y. The second is an editorial from the same paper of September 18, 1862. The third — Miss IMILDA WENDELL's letter to her brother, on hearing of his enlistment — was published near the period of its date in the *Morning Herald* of Utica, N. Y.]

I.

Among the many brave men sacrificed upon the altar of their country, in the great fight of Chancellorsville, we notice the name of NELSON O. WENDELL, Captain of Co. F, 121st Reg. N. Y. S. Volunteers — who fell on Salem Heights, near Fredericksburg, on the 3d of May, 1863.

Mr. Wendell was born in Warren, Herkimer Co., N. Y., April 6, 1832, and at his death was but little over 31 years of age. He was a young man of fine address, commanding person, patriotic impulses and good literary acquirements. After fitting himself in the rudimental branches, in the schools of his native state, he went west and graduated at Hanover College, Indiana. Being dependent upon his own efforts, he afterwards engaged in teaching, and met with considerable success in that profession, in Kentucky and Missouri. Impaired health obliged him to relinquish so confining a business for a time, when he returned to this state, and was soon thereafter appointed School Commissioner in Otsego county and located at Cooperstown. A restoration of his health found him again at his chosen avocation, a professor in the West Winfield Academy — where he was employed when the Elsworth (44th N. Y.) Regiment was being formed. The citizens of West Winfield happily united upon Mr. Wendell, to represent said town in that Regiment — and he yielded with alacrity his position in the school, to respond to the call of a bleeding country. How well that confidence was reposed, and how faithfully and heroically his services were rendered, are attested by his bravery in some eight or ten battles, and the final sacrifice of his valuable life.

In illustration of the earnest determination with which he entered battle, we give an extract from a letter to his brother, written immediately after receiving marching orders, and while preparing to cross the Rappahannock with Sedgwick's Corps, on the 28th of April, 1863. He says:

"We have marching orders for 3 P. M., this day. Destination, Fredericksburg and the heights beyond. A fearful crash of arms and bloody contest will ensue; but we are in fine spirits and confident of success. If I survive, you shall soon hear from me again. If I am slain, be assured I die in a good cause."

Also, in concluding a letter to W. C. Wendell, a nephew in Albany, he adds:

"But should I fall, remember that I die in the full faith of the justice and ultimate success of our cause."

At an earlier date — some time in February last — in answer to a letter from his brother, Jacob Wendell, Esq., begging him to procure a furlough and visit his home — he sent the following characteristic response:

ARMY OF THE POTOMAC,
CAMP OF THE 121ST N. Y.,
NEAR WHITE OAK CHURCH, VA.,
February 26, 1863.

* * * * * You ask me to make you a visit — thank you for the invitation — but I must decline the honor. I am a soldier, and shall soldier it till I die — am killed or wounded — dismissed — or the war ends. This is no half-way work with me. I do not wish to taste the pleasure of civil life till my work is done, and I can freely and fully indulge without expectation of returning to the field. I am now happy, and do not wish to do anything to render my situation unpleasant, which emerging into the outer world might do. I am now like a man shut out from the world, and since I have become so used to this mode of life, I do not want to return till I go to stay.

I entered this struggle with my whole soul — forgetful of aught else. I always had a veneration for the old flag. It has brought tears to my eyes on the eve of many a battle, to see the flag bow to a passing general, and to see him so gracefully and with such dignity return the salute. Would death or wounds on that day have been unwelcome? Would the gaping cannon, or the rattling musketry, have shaken for a moment my resolution? I am not my own, my life is my country's. I have wedded her cause, and all else, every past fault, sorrow and regret, is forgotten — buried in the deepest, darkest oblivion, by the supreme satisfaction I now feel — the happiness I now enjoy, in defending the flag I venerate, in serving the country I love.

I know my patriotism is not of the flashy kind, my zeal not effervescent. It is substantial — permanent — growing. All private griefs are forgotten, never again to be revived. I die in the service or come out a new man.

No, I cannot go home, even if I knew how badly you wanted to see me. I do know, but my acts shall never belie my words. I feel, talk, and shall show my zeal whenever I see a rebel in arms — that hideous deformity of human nature! May God forgive me if they are brothers.   Truly Yours,
  N. O. WENDELL.

Such words could never have been written or uttered by one who was incapable of appreciating and performing his responsibilities, or who had left his heart behind him. Though first enlisted as a private in the 44th, he was soon promoted to a Sergeant, and as early as August, 1862, he obtained a Captain's Commission, and was transferred to the 121st. These prompt promotions were the reward of manifest worth, earned by soldierly deportment — fervently attested to by letters of condolence to his kindred, from his surviving comrades. The officer subsequently in command of Co. F, in a letter to Col. Jacob Wendell, under date " Near White Oak Church, Va., May 12, 1863," pays the following tribute :

" The Captain (your brother) fell on Sunday afternoon, May 3d, near the close of the hottest and bloodiest engagement of this desolating war, while gallantly leading and cheering on his valiant little band. The 121st played the most conspicuous part in the bloody drama of the day, but all the laurels won, were bought by the lives of many a hero and patriot soldier. I did not observe the Captain at the moment he fell, but those who did, take pride and pleasure in paying to his gallantry and heroism the most distinguished honor and praise. He fell, cheering his brave men on to more glorious achievements for their country, doing his perilous duty like a true patriot and brave soldier. He was shot through the head, as the battle was about drawing to a close, and was doubtless instantly killed. * * * His death has shed a gloom over the whole regiment; a bright light seems to have gone out forever ; a kindly, cheerful voice has been hushed in the solemn silence of the tomb, and more than five hundred soldiers' hearts beat heavily in view of his fate." * * *

Capt. Jno. D. Fish, of the same regiment, thus concludes a letter : " In the fight, he showed himself brave, gallant, and fell while fully and fearlessly facing the foe."

To these testimonials might be added many others, equally eulogistic. But, while they might be gratifying to the personal friends, they are not needed to embalm the heroic conduct of the departed, in the performance of a noble work, like that of saving our glorious Union. Although " man dies, his memory lives."

II.

MERITED PROMOTION.— We are permitted to publish a letter this week from Nelson O. Wendell, a late private in the 44th N. Y., to his brother, Col. Wendell, of this village. The exposure and endurance therein set forth, as well as the incidental bravery, have been more than confirmed by Col. Rice, commanding the Regiment. That colonel strongly recommended Mr. Wendell to the governor for promotion, upon which a Captain's commission was issued on the 18th of August, but was not received until the 5th instant. He was at once honorably discharged from the 44th, and transferred to lead Co. F, 121st N. Y. Regiment, commanded by Col. Franchot.

We have such abiding faith in the policy of taking our officers from the ranks, and promoting those whose pluck and worth have been demonstrated in battle, that this instance of favorable recognition is worthy of mention. While the act is a just requital of merit, it also acts as a stimulant to the rank and file whose lives are perilled for their country. We are therefore glad to hear of Mr. Wendell's good luck, and know that he will honor the commission entrusted to him.

CENTERVILLE, Va., Sept. 1, 1862.

J. WENDELL, Esq.,

DEAR BROTHER: I have time and strength but for a few words; but to relieve you and the friends of unnecessary uneasiness on my account, I will just say that, though we were again in the hottest of the fight on Saturday the 30th ult., I am out of it safely for the fifth time, but completely exhausted by sickness, exposure, long and rapid marches, and continuous skirmishing and fighting during the last two weeks. But there is no use in complaining; as long as a man can stand up, he must do his duty; and I do mine most cheerfully. Our Reg't (the 44th N. Y. V.) now numbers but 87 men fit for duty. We shall probably soon retire to Washington, fresh troops taking our places. Before God, my conscience is clear in having done my whole duty to my country. Out of three companies, that were out skirmishing, I was the only member who advanced to the charge, with the Brigade that came to our relief. It was a desperate fight, and a disastrous retreat. May God have mercy on the country. I verily believe, however, that we shall soon be chasing the rebels hotly back to Richmond.

I remain as ever,

Yours for the Union,

NELSON O. WENDELL.

III.

WEST BEND, Wis., Aug. 25, 1861.

NELSON O. WENDELL, Esq.,

Ellsworth Regiment, Albany Barracks, N. Y.,

DEAR BROTHER: You may form an opinion as to our surprise on learning of your enlistment, but you can scarcely imagine how great is the anxiety felt by us all, in view of the dangers and hardships you may have to encounter and endure, and which must almost of necessity fall to your lot, in leading the life of a soldier. In view of these stern facts, you have caused a shade of gloom to cast its sombre veil over the hearts of your many friends, notwithstanding the conviction we all have, that you are but doing your whole duty. We all fully realize the important necessity for every one of the brave sons of our once glorious Union, to buckle on his armor, and go forth at once to the rescue of the constitution, her laws, her honor, and her institutions, and to labor, toil, suffer, and perchance to die, for her preservation. Especially is it a duty, when we know full well it is jeopardized by the dishonor and treachery of her own ungrateful sons. We honor you for this practical evidence of your loyalty and courage, in this her hour of need, and that you love your country, and are ready and willing to defend her institutions before any and every other consideration. Hence I cannot wish you back, although my heart and feelings oftentimes sadly rebel against my sense of right and justice.

Now, dear brother, when you think of your far off sister, and know that she wishes you to be a good and brave soldier, think also what would be her feelings should you by rashness or carelessness fall on the field of battle. I can only add, God bless and preserve you, and return you in safety to your friends and relatives; and to this end rest assured that you shall ever have the prayers of your sister. Most affectionately,

IMILDA WENDELL.

www.ingramcontent.com/pod-product-compliance
Lightning Source LLC
Chambersburg PA
CBHW031444160426
43195CB00010BB/838